D0442295

Praise for *Well Connected*

"If you want to turn your networking activities into a predictable process with measurable results, read *Well Connected*."
  —**David Stone**, CEO and cofounder, CashStar.com

"Curtis's *Well Connected* framework provides the structure for leveraging your connections selectively. Today, more so than ever, networking is about quality, not quantity."
  —**Gisele E. Garceau**, senior human capital strategist, EMC Corporation

"In our hyper-networked world, managers who read *Well Connected* will find its practical advice invaluable for success."
  —**Amit Mukherjee**, author, *The Spider's Strategy*, and president, Ishan Advisors

"Given the flurry of 'networking activity' driven by today's social media trends, *Well Connected* is a timely and welcome read. Curtis forces readers to be both thoughtful and strategic about how they connect with others. *Well Connected* will help you increase your networking success."
  —**Melissa Raffoni**, president, Raffoni CEO Consulting

"Surviving—and thriving—as a leader in business is all about connecting with others. *Well Connected* is a well-considered, practical book—and couldn't be more timely. The case studies resonate and make this a useful and enjoyable read, something all too rare in business books."
  —**Joe Knowles**, executive director, Institute for Health Metrics

"Curtis's *Well Connected* is a must-read for anyone who doesn't have the time to network the 'old way.'"
  —**Robert Picardi**, CEO, Raid, Inc.

"Curtis's *Well Connected* approach to networking enabled GiveUsYourPoor.org to connect to new board members, partners, and funders who were passionate and perfect fits for our organization. His approach is easy to replicate and will help you succeed, too."
  —**John McGah**, managing director,
    GiveUsYourPoor.org

"This is not 'Networking 101.' Curtis's Right Person–Right Approach method brings the art and science of making productive business and career connections to a new level. I'm hard-pressed to think of anyone who wouldn't benefit from *Well Connected*."
  —**Sandy Lipson**, executive recruiting and
    organization development consultant, and
    former vice president of talent management,
    Fidelity Investments

"I have worked with thousands of executives and professionals over the years, building collaborative communities and customer programs. In one book, Gordon has captured the principles that took me a decade to figure out. The Right Person–Right Approach method in *Well Connected* is right on the money. It removes the wasted effort from social networking and replaces it with results."
  —**Mark S. Bonchek**, founder and CEO, Collaborative Revolution and Truman Company

WELL CONNECTED

An Unconventional Approach to Building
GENUINE, EFFECTIVE BUSINESS RELATIONSHIPS

GORDON S. CURTIS
with
GREG LEWIS

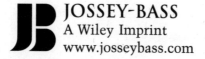

JOSSEY-BASS
A Wiley Imprint
www.josseybass.com

Published by Jossey-Bass
A Wiley Imprint
989 Market Street, San Francisco, CA 94103-1741—www.josseybass.com

Jossey-Bass books and products are available through most bookstores. To contact Jossey-Bass directly call our Customer Care Department within the U.S. at 800-956-7739, outside the U.S. at 317-572-3986, or fax 317-572-4002.

Jossey-Bass also publishes its books in a variety of electronic formats. Some content that appears in print may not be available in electronic books.

Library of Congress Cataloging-in-Publication Data
Curtis, Gordon S.
    Well connected : an unconventional approach to building genuine, effective business relationships / Gordon S. Curtis with Greg Lewis.
        p. cm.
    Includes index.
    ISBN 978-0-470-57794-3 (hardback); ISBN 978-0-470-64232-7 (ebk);
    ISBN 978-0-470-64234-3 (ebk); ISBN 978-0-64233-5 (ebk)
    1. Strategic alliances (Business) 2. Business networks. 3. Interpersonal relations. I. Lewis, Greg. II. Title.
    HD69.S8C87 2010
    650.1'3—dc22

                                        2010013841

Printed in the United States of America
FIRST EDITION
HB Printing   10 9 8 7 6 5 4 3 2 1

To my loving wife, Bobbie,
and our children, Lydia and Will
—G.S.C.

For Catharine
—G.L.

CONTENTS

WELL

CONNECTED

CHAPTER 1

Redefining Networking for the Twenty-First Century

- *"I just don't have a year to spend getting up to speed to do*
- *my job," David told me. David had hired me as an*
- *executive coach to help him accelerate his adaptation to a*
- *newly landed position. Instead of the few big and easily*
- *located potential customers he was accustomed to dealing*
- *with for his former employer, he now had to find the best*
- *prospects among a field of thousands of superficially similar*
- *businesses.*
- *Rather than target each potential customer individually*
- *or take a shotgun approach (broadcasting what he needed*
- *across his whole network), we focused on identifying the one*
- *key person he would choose to help enable him to*
- *accomplish his goal. The first step was to identify precisely*
- *what information he needed—one of the standard questions*
- *in the* Right Person–Right Approach method, *which in*
- *this case was "Who are the best potential customers in the*
- *new territory?"—to carry out his proposed strategy in*
- *the fastest and most efficient manner. (The Right Person–Right*
- *Approach method is at the heart of this book.) That led*

us to ask, "Who makes a business of knowing who the top performers in the industry are?" We followed that up with "How can I get that person to share that knowledge with me?"

"This seems impossible," David told me when I introduced the idea. "If it were that easy, everybody would be doing it."

I replied, "Well, it's easy if you know how to do it—but it is impossible if you don't have the strategy, plan, and concept!"

The method we employed involved profiling potential contacts to determine who would be most likely to have exactly the right set of knowledge, relationships, personal characteristics, abilities, and inclination to provide the information David needed to narrow down and access the sea of prospects. But how do you find someone like that? Inspired and guided by the notion that such a person existed, David asked industry colleagues to advise him about who (1) had the knowledge he needed and (2) showed evidence of a disposition to connect with others. As he framed his questions in those terms, he realized he actually knew the answer himself already; his screening confirmed this insight. He then knew he likely had the right person in his sights.

After that, we designed an approach to the contact that would virtually ensure willingness to share what amounted to proprietary information. This was feasible because David had been able, through his research, to determine precisely how he could motivate his contact through offering something of perceived value in exchange for cooperation. At first, David thought it audacious to approach such a person with

- *such a request. But he soon learned that people could have*
- *very good reasons for sharing information with him.*
- *Bottom line: Much to the amazement of his manage-*
- *ment, David was successful in acquiring the hidden informa-*
- *tion he needed to narrow the field of potential clients from*
- *thousands down to thirty of the most qualified. This dramati-*
- *cally shortened his learning curve and accelerated his time-to-*
- *performance. Within his first six months at a new job in an*
- *unfamiliar sector of his industry, David was able to become*
- *one of the top performers, and doubled his earnings.*

Why Does It Look So Easy?

Some people seem to be able to achieve their business objectives easily. Some people seem to find new jobs effortlessly—and very quickly to boot—whenever they want them. And others can raise funds when they need to do so, even when equally deserving entrepreneurs and charities fail. Is it really that easy for them? Or are they just profiting by blind luck?

Sometimes luck does play a part. But—like David—you can make your own luck, and then reaching your goals is easy, or at any rate a quick process, free of wasted energy. There's a saying: *Luck is when opportunity meets preparation.* Well, it is even more true with the approach outlined in this book.

The key is to selectively engage the right people, making sure you're not simply connected to them, but *well-connected*. If you do this carefully and thoughtfully in service of honest goals—in pursuit of work or opportunities where you can in fact deliver what you promise—you will not only succeed in achieving your career or business goals, but you will also slice months, even years, off the time it normally takes people to achieve such goals.

Using the Right Person–Right Approach method:

- Busy executives with barely a few hours a week to devote to networking have streamlined the networking process and worked so efficiently that they've succeeded in spite of their busy schedules.

- Shy, introverted people who were uncomfortable asking others to meet with them have managed to present their talents and their assets so compellingly that the people they originally hesitated to approach were now asking *them* for meetings.

- Inexperienced students just out of school have convinced people in high places to work with them to achieve their early career objectives.

Once people learn the Right Person–Right Approach method, they don't go back to their old ways. Unlike so many new approaches or new grips or new swings, it is easy to put into practice. And all you need is one 450-yard drive to lock that experience into your networking memory. It is a reliable relationship-building road map for those seeking to achieve virtually any business or career goal; for example:

- Gathering critical market research and intelligence
- Generating client referrals

- Fundraising
- Performing a job search
- Making hiring and other personnel decisions
- Engineering a career change
- Performing due diligence
- Preparing for and engaging in interviews and negotiations
- Selecting vendors
- Making the transition into a new role or job
- Speeding up the sales process

Tasks like these come up over and over in the course of a career, some of them every day. From attorneys to research scientists, from entrepreneurs to managers, from veterans to rookies, the Right Person–Right Approach method provides a framework that enables people to precisely articulate objectives, find someone who can provide real help in carrying them out, and engage that person's interest in support of their goals.

What's Wrong with Networking Now?

As unemployment rises and prospects for increasing sales or raising capital grow scarcer, the element of fear can creep in. In the last few years, almost everyone has felt it, and people everywhere are looking for ways to help alleviate it. Meanwhile, employers have been asking their people to become more resourceful, to do more with less, and to do it with a smile.

The best way to succeed in such a demanding and hypercompetitive environment is to make partnerships—synergies with colleagues, with vendors, with competitors, with anyone who might share a common goal and can help build mutual success. Such partnerships require strong, meaningful relationships, but networking to build real relationships is becoming a lost art just when it is becoming more and more widely viewed as the key to success in the twenty-first century, even in fields far removed from sales and other areas where human interactions are at the forefront.

For example, years ago when Stephen R. Covey cited a study about the performance of engineers with Bell Labs/Lucent, the researchers had found that the most successful engineers were the ones who reached out most to internal and external helpers, often picking up the insights they needed to complete a project within a day. (Others took rather longer than a day to work out the solution on their own, and some never did so.) This difference was so marked that success levels correlated with access to other people with relevant knowledge—and not with experience or education in engineering.

And Jeff Dyer and Hal Gregersen, the grad school professors who run the "Innovator's DNA" Web site (http://innovatorsdna.com), agree. Among the key skills that make innovators stand out from the crowd, they list "finding and testing ideas through a network of diverse individuals to get radically different perspectives"—that is, networking.

Prior to the Internet–cell phone–immediate and universal access revolution, networking was largely accomplished one to one, with a view to establishing mutually beneficial and lasting relationships. What passes for social networking in the business world today has almost nothing to do with that. Instead, it is increasingly about accumulating as many connections as possible via Twitter and LinkedIn and Facebook and similar social networking sites (SNSs). More and more people are spending more and more time texting and instant-messaging and tweeting and linking their way through the day in the fond belief that all this effort enhances their social networks.

Don't get me wrong. Online social networking is here to stay, and it can be very valuable; it just doesn't serve well as your only form of networking. Why? This new and rapidly changing networking environment has created a situation in which many people are scrambling to connect with as many others as they can, in whatever ways they can, in an effort to promote a "personal brand" and thus stand out from an increasingly large crowd in an increasingly competitive environment. But all this effort is producing little by way of measurable results. Increasing the number of contacts in a virtual network tends to come at the expense of building mutually beneficial relationships with specific people. It is too easy to indulge in one-to-many messages and bypass the more difficult—and often difficult-to-justify—time-intensive exchanges that lead to real connection and exchange of measurable value.

Unfortunately, the pure friend-link-and-tweet school of social networking makes it all too easy to reduce your chances of achieving your career and business objectives rather than enhance them. Of course, it can and does produce results for people, but it leaves too much to chance. Incautious broadcast networking can contaminate your network, as you will shoot yourself in the foot if you are unclear about what you want and why you are worthy of help, or you approach people in a one-way exchange, or both.

Much of the communication and so-called networking that takes place on social networking Web sites consists of what Scott Berkun identifies as nothing more than "noise." As he explains in a blog entry charmingly titled "Calling Bullshit on Social Media," the majority of this activity involves "people forwarding things they were forwarded that almost none of them appear to have read." These eager forwarders seem to think that frequency and quantity are the most important qualities in their communications with their networks. What they don't realize is that their untargeted attempts at connecting with others quickly and impersonally can become annoying at best—and a liability at worst. If you say the wrong things to the wrong people at the wrong times often enough, it won't be long before you turn them off—permanently—to the point where they'll remember your name for all the wrong reasons.

Not that there's any built-in problem with promoting your brand and developing a large number of Internet "friends." You don't have to stay away from social networking sites; they're playing an important role in how people connect with each other these days. But more often than not, this casual, virtual approach will not help you achieve your specific business and career objectives.

Not always—as the saying goes, "Even a blind pig finds an occasional acorn"—but broadcasting your profile to others you've come to know remotely through the Internet produces results only sporadically. Although it may feel exciting to engage in the online social networking scramble, you don't need to hunt blindly: there's a much better way to get what you want. The Right Person–Right Approach method will teach you how to target your messages so that virtually every one of them communicates something important and meaningful—and goes to specific people in your network rather than being broadcast far and wide. But beyond that, it will teach you the strategies and techniques to be successful in achieving your business and career goals in the shortest possible time.

What Is the Right Person—Right Approach Method?

The Right Person–Right Approach method for using social networks to achieve business and career objectives grew out of my consulting practice, which is unique in many ways. I'm an executive coach *and* an agent. That is, rather than simply advising people how to progress, I also serve a role much like that of a sports agent, helping put clients in front of the right enablers and decision makers and working with them right through to the point where they close the deal and secure the partner, funding, job, client, or whatever goal they are pursuing.

Taking on both of these roles means that I put my own relationship capital on the line with every one of my clients. Of the many definitions out there, I prefer the one that regards *relationship capital* as the store of goodwill that builds up between contacts and associates through mutually beneficial exchanges. The need to preserve relationship capital means that I've had to develop a framework that works every time; after all, many of the people my clients engage with are either already valuable parts of my network or potential additions to it, and—as I've learned to my cost—any misstep will lead to erosion of key relationships. So I get a lot of practice in helping to identify exactly the right person for someone to talk to and in guiding people to exactly the right approach, so that both parties achieve an outcome that's mutually beneficial.

All this isn't something I was taught or that I do by instinct, though I did start out with a strong desire to make connections—that is, to introduce everyone to everyone else. I learned networking the hard way.

After starting out in the executive search industry, I decided to move into outplacement—not only was it steadier work, but it was also better suited to my temperament. I'd discovered that I was a closet coach. In executive search, you're supposed to be more transactional than relational (and I say this with the utmost respect for my many search colleagues); the idea is to find the best candidate for the job and then move on, without trying to coach anyone on career development, and for sure without trying to coach anyone you've already placed. If the fee was paid and the guarantee was up, it was all over. No more hand-holding. But I couldn't resist spending inordinate amounts of time advising people, even though my boss frowned on it, so I had to do it in hiding.

Executive outplacement, by contrast, took the opposite view—to help the person find the job, you had to be willing to do some work on the person, too. In other words, it was a business that actually paid people to do what I was sneaking into my practice.

So I did the logical thing: I went to the Directory of Executive Outplacement Consulting Firms (www. Kennedyinfo.com), listed all the best outplacement firms, and then asked my dad, Elliot—who was with the management consulting firm Harbridge House—whether he knew anyone who could help me get in to talk to any of them. He told me to call one of his friends at the search firm Korn Ferry, who likely knew people in the business.

So I called the guy, identified myself, and said, "Hey, my dad said you might be able to help me. Do you know anybody at these companies?" I reeled off the list. He thought a minute and lobbed me a referral to Warren Radtke, founding principal and managing director of Right Management Consulting's Boston Office—the most successful office out of one hundred worldwide. I'd identified Right Management as one of the firms I really wanted to work for.

I phoned Radtke and told him I'd like to work for his company. It was my lucky day; I later realized that he was humoring me—he could surely tell by my voice and approach that I was a wet-behind-the-ears young guy—but he agreed to see me. I thought I was Super Networking

Man—three connections and in! I was already picturing my office, with my feet up on the desk.

But when I met with him, as soon as we got past the pleasantries, five minutes into the interview, my ego began to shrink. Radtke peppered me with question after question about the outplacement industry, about his company, about the kinds of things I expected to do in the job I was seeking—and I didn't know jack. After letting me squirm for a few minutes, he put *his* feet up on his desk and said, "Kid, when you have learned everything you can possibly learn about the outplacement business, the forces that are driving the business, the technologies that are shaping the future of the business, the economics that are affecting the business, all of my competitors and how they differentiate themselves from one another, the sources of information you need to know about the business, and the thought leaders in the industry, then give me a call and maybe we can talk some more."

And that was one of the biggest favors anyone has ever done for me. Not that I recognized it at the time, of course. I slunk out of Warren Radtke's office like a dog with its tail between its legs, wondering how I could ever face my dad or his friend who'd given me the referral. How could I tell them what had happened? Well, it finally occurred to me: I could concentrate on the bright side—he hadn't told me to get lost; he'd told me to do some stuff and get back to him—and that was all anybody else needed to know. Besides, maybe taking that attitude would even do me some good. That was my true nature reasserting itself—as one boss often assured me, I'm a delusionary optimist.

Anyway, as soon as I got home, I began to call anyone I could think of who knew anything at all about the out-placement industry. Hundreds of calls later (remember, I was a recruiter; I already had a cauliflower ear from that job's required hundred-plus calls per day), I managed to land meetings with twenty-one people who were will-ing, if not necessarily able, to help me try to bone up on the intelligence I needed to gather so I could go back to Radtke and request another meeting with a straight face.

Did that get me what I needed? Hardly. Outplacement wasn't all I didn't know jack about—I also didn't know how to screen these people to find out if they would be able to provide the right information, so I just talked to all the ones who would talk to me and asked for whatever they felt like offering. And for a long time, I didn't even come close to accomplishing my objective.

Again, the sheer volume of my aimless, misdirected, and unfocused calls—which I could make based on my hard-earned experience—was my only advantage here.

The first twenty people I begged for help responded by telling stories and doling out little bits of data, none of which came together and added up to anything useful. Finally, and basically by accident, I got lucky again. I wound up sitting across a desk from Ginny Rehberg—president and CEO of Rehberg Management Group, a Boston-area executive coaching, outplacement, and career consulting firm—who happened to be exactly the person I needed to talk to. She had the information and the contacts I was looking for, and she was willing to sit down with me and give me what she knew (and I didn't) that I needed.

She said, essentially, "OK, here's who you need to call and here's what you need to know, and here's exactly how to approach them to demonstrate that you know everything you would be expected to counsel their client about." She spent more than an hour and a half with me, and at the end of our meeting I had seven names. More important, I knew enough about what each of those seven people had to offer that I could ask them the right questions. Over the next month, I managed to gather the intelligence I needed.

I finally mustered up the audacity to circle back to Warren Radtke again. Well aware that I had been given a rare second chance in this world of job interviewing, I knew this was my last shot. I asked for the second meeting he'd (sort of) said he would grant me. When we got together, I thanked him for the exercise. "Here's the information you recommended I find out about the industry," I told him, proceeding to present a thorough report as scripted by Ginny. Then I said, "And here's a list of companies you don't have as clients, and here's what I think you need to do to get them as clients, and here are all the decision makers at those companies who will return my call within twenty hours."

He offered me a job on the spot. This despite the fact that I'd been told over and over that I was much too young to be coaching executives and professionals. No one could believe that I'd been hired for that job. If they only knew— it was by pure luck and an inordinate amount of wasted energy that I got it.

Now that I knew firsthand how much of a difference it could make, I began to keep a close eye on the successes and the failures of my own networking attempts and those of my clients and the hundreds of networkers I was advising and watching. Radtke's company had me conducting a series of professional networking workshops where executives shared their goals and attempted to find contacts who would lead them to the jobs they were looking for, and that became the start of my own research. In the course of observing many such meetings and thinking over what people said and how they reacted to others in the group, I was astonished at the number of weak introductions and lame summaries I was hearing from people who thought they were eloquently stating their needs.

The real moment-of-truth experience—the one that helped me really see how bad most networking attempts were—was when I was a guest speaker for the leading executive networking organization, Execunet. After I spoke, I participated in their standard networking breakout session. It was painful to watch.

The questions seemed simple enough: "Where have you been? Where are you going? And how can we help?" The answers to the last question were vague and uniform, boiling down to versions of "Increase my network in order to find a new position." Few offered to share much in the way of contacts and referrals. Instead, they mainly went on to ask, "Does anyone know of a company looking for a CEO [or a COO or a CFO]?" Predictably, when asked for information in this way, the group would respond with a collective head shake (palpably thinking, "If I did, I'd be there instead of here!"), and the would-be executive would sit down and watch the next person go through the same pitiful process. They were all wasting their time in the meeting, probably not talking to the right people and certainly not taking the right approach. But it was considered best-practice networking at the time.

Who's the Right Person? What's the Right Approach?

As I started working with individual clients, a pattern emerged. When an introduction or referral led to a hugely successful outcome, the parties could be described in these terms:

- *Knowledgeable:* Successful networkers knew what they wanted and were talking to contacts who had the exact knowledge or relationships they needed.

- *Inclined:* Successful meetings were with contacts who understood the value of investing time helping other people.

- *Available:* Successful connections required the follow-through to deliver—not just a promise to do so that never translated into finding time for a meeting.

- *Like-minded:* Successful exchanges began with a real connection—some commonality between the networker and the contact.

- *Obligated:* Successful requests for assistance happened when the contact felt an obligation based on a referral or some previous association with the networker.

- *Motivated:* Successful requests for assistance required more than a sense of obligation, however; the networker still needed to offer the contact a reason to go out of the way to help, to stimulate their willingness to help.

- *Able:* Successful outcomes happened only when both sides managed to do what was needed; the contact had to be able to present their inquiry in a form the networker could grasp, and the networker had to be able to accept help.

If one or more of these features wasn't present, an introduction was likely to fail. That was an important realization for me: often it's not necessarily what you *do* that creates a negative outcome, but rather what you *don't* do. As the framework developed further, I realized that the success of an introduction was essentially certain if all of the criteria in the framework were satisfied. As I gave up my early (delusional) optimism that everyone should meet everyone else, my success rates began to climb significantly, as did those of my clients. Instead of their ranks including some pleased clients and some wondering what I was possibly thinking when facilitating an introduction, more and more felt that each introduction was a winner.

And I started to gain a reputation for making introductions that produced explosively positive results both for my clients and for those they met with. People talked about "lightning strikes events" and "blockbuster introductions."

Why did this happen and keep happening? Those I coached weren't reaching out ill-prepared and at random, the way I had after Radtke fed me my ignorance—they were carefully selecting the right people to talk to. And they weren't following the old "here is everything I've ever done" pitch, or "I'll take anything you can give me" inquiry either. They were finding out what they had to offer as it related to the specific needs and interests of specific contacts and approaching them with a value proposition up-front, establishing that the proposed interview would be worthwhile for the interviewee as a matter of self-interest and not as simple charity.

That developed into the Right Person–Right Approach method (the name I've used for it ever since). The Right Person–Right Approach method is sometimes described as contrarian, and in an important sense, it is just that: it suggests that if you want to build relationships and achieve career and business objectives, you don't need to expand your networks until you're connected to thousands of people in the hope that one of them will help you. Instead, you need to find the one right person who can fulfill that role, who can enable you to achieve a specific objective.

I call that right person—and there's at least one for every viable business objective—a *critical enabler*. For a productive and mutually beneficial exchange, a critical enabler must, first and foremost, be (1) knowledgeable; that is, must know things or people that you need to know or reach and cannot get to on your own without a great deal of time-consuming and frustrating research in unfamiliar territory. A critical enabler also needs to be (2) inclined to assist you, (3) available to offer help, and (4) preferably like-minded as well—that is, someone who has something in common with you. These four factors seem obvious when stated in so many words, but in practice they're remarkably easy to neglect unless you sit down and focus on them specifically.

Identifying the right person is not enough, however. You also need to make your approach in the right way so as to develop a real connection with them—to be *well-connected*. The foundation of the right-approach component of the framework is a concept I call *progressive reciprocity*. A gesture of progressive reciprocity is an up-front gesture, an offer of something of genuine value to the other party, set out before you ask something for yourself in return. This offer says, "I'm not your typical one-way networker who is just out to get what I can from you and then bolt without offering something in return." It's the antidote to what I call *obligatory reciprocity*—the widespread practice of halfheartedly offering to help someone out *after* you've asked them to help you—which I see out there all the time in most business exchanges.

Human nature plays a big role in the Right Person–Right Approach method. For instance, although many people tend to hold their networks close to their chests, the Right Person–Right Approach framework makes it possible to identify specific kinds of people likely to be willing to open their networks and provide information that will help you achieve your business and career goals. When you lead with what you might have to offer and you clearly describe what you need, you open up new ways to make contact with the people who otherwise wouldn't be motivated to help you or even know how to do so.

The method works well enough that I've begun to write language into my coaching agreements that says, in effect, "I guarantee that you're going to be able to walk away from every deliberate networking effort with tangible, measurable results if you employ the principles of the Right Person–Right Approach method." That is, these days I promise every one of my clients that they'll get a *bona fide* lead or useful piece of intelligence from almost every person they contact using this method, as compared to perhaps one out of twenty using conventional approaches. That's how much I believe in it; that's how reliable I know it to be.

One of the things I hear repeatedly from my clients is that they've rediscovered their "networking confidence" or discovered confidence they never thought they could have. They've finally found something that lets them feel confident and excited that they're going to succeed virtually every time they reach out to people who can help them get where they want to go.

So What Does It All Mean?

To sum up, over the past decade or so—with the enormous explosion of electronic connectivity—people have largely lost sight of one of the most important reasons for networking: to connect on a fundamental level with other people through value exchanges. It is true that something quite extraordinary has been gained through this almost infinite electronic interconnectability, but something important has been lost in the process.

But not irrevocably lost. The framework in this book will enable you to reestablish old contacts and spark new contacts with a select group of knowledgeable people with whom you share a common value as the most important aspect of effective and fruitful networking. It emphasizes the measurable *quality* and not the *quantity* of your relationships in an era in which people too often mistake the fact that they can have 1,722 online "friends," none of whom they really know, for value-based networking.

The following chapters outline, step by step, how to use the Right Person–Right Approach to accomplish your business objective effectively and efficiently. I encourage you to use *Well Connected* as a practical handbook and to identify one of your own specific career or business objectives early in your reading of the book and follow it through the process as you read. When you've completed this book, you'll have that same confidence. You'll have a road map to guide you through every critical career decision, from whom to hire to what vendor to choose to how to raise capital, and you'll have a blueprint for success in making every critical future career transition and achieving every key business goal.

CHAPTER 2

Prep Work

RETHINKING YOUR NETWORKING STRATEGY

- ### USING A SHOTGUN
- *Joseph was CEO of a company that was developing computer-*
- *ized robotic devices that promised to solve a number of problems*
- *that search and rescue teams and security personnel deal with*
- *on a daily basis. He needed funding to expand his manufactur-*
- *ing operations and move his product closer to being released.*
-
- *Joseph's networking strategy was built on his highly outgoing*
- *personality and his readiness to pitch his business plan wherever*
- *and whenever he saw the opportunity. He had managed to con-*
- *tact principals from close to fifty different venture capital firms,*
- *but he hadn't been able to get beyond a phone call or first meet-*
- *ing with any of them. His networking approach—what and*
- *how he was communicating and whom he was communicating*
- *with—had led him down several dead-end paths, and he wor-*
- *ried that he was running out of prospects to fund his company.*
-
- ### WRITE AND WAIT
- *Jane had an advanced degree and had demonstrated her*
- *capabilities working in research labs at two different com-*
- *panies. Now her current company was downsizing, and she*

needed to find another job. Prior to the announcement, she had thought her job was secure, and—not being a natural extrovert—she had neglected to build and maintain a network. As a result, she had very few industry contacts outside her company.

Jane had already tried the traditional approach in her job search. She'd identified a group of ten prospective employers, and she'd sent a résumé, along with a plain-vanilla cover e-mail, to each of their HR directors. She'd also responded to several online job postings. Unfortunately, this traditional strategy produced the traditional results: despite her excellent qualifications, she had not received a single callback, much less a job interview. Her networking strategy, which was built on her naturally reticent personality, was making her job search very difficult.

Less Haste, More Progress

Both Joseph and Jane were feeling somewhat desperate in my initial meetings with them. They knew they weren't making progress toward their goals, and the first thing each of them said they wanted to do was "get started right away." I told them, "Slow down. We have to do a little prep work first. Eventually you'll be able to use the Right Person–Right Approach method instinctively, but first you need to learn a few things about yourself and your networking strategy."

It's natural to have a networking strategy: a way of approaching (or, in some cases, not approaching) and communicating with others—in fact, you can't avoid it. This default networking strategy is at work whether you're dealing with your contacts face to face, through e-mail and telephone calls, or via social networking Web sites. In these everyday networking interactions, you've developed habits—behaviors that you repeat over and over as you relate to others in your networks. Over time, these habits have come to form your networking strategy.

Why Can't We Just Get Started?

Your personal networking strategy has probably seemed to be serving you well, at least until you reached a critical point in your career or job responsibilities where you needed to get results right away. That point might be a job search necessitated by your company's downsizing, a business or funding opportunity that you sense might be slipping away, or the need to quickly gather information for a project with a very tight time line or to get yourself on board with a new boss, job, project, or company. Suddenly you're faced with a challenge and your tried-and-true networking strategy is not getting you the results you need. Like Joseph and Jane, when you're in a situation like this and speed seems to be of the essence, you probably don't want to hear "slow down," or "let's evaluate your networking strategy."

But slowing down is just what you need to do—if only for a short time. Like Joseph's and Jane's, your personality may have led you to adopt a specific approach to networking. But because it's highly likely that something about that approach is keeping you from getting optimum results, the first thing you must do is take time to examine your networking strategy and see how it's holding you back from achieving your goals. This is useful even if you have been getting enough positive feedback to make it feel as though your strategy is pretty good already—because unless you're getting something you really need from at least nine out of ten of your inquiries or requests for referrals, there's room for improvement. If you're like most people in these situations and are not getting the outcomes you want, you need to analyze how you're approaching others, measure the results you're getting, and make changes that will guarantee that you achieve success.

You don't need to try to change your personality. If you're naturally somewhat shy and reticent, you don't need to morph into an outgoing, life-of-the-party type—or vice versa. Even if your personal tendencies have led you into some unproductive networking habits, the Right Person–Right Approach framework will enable you to change those habits without changing who you are as a person. You don't need to turn yourself into Gordon Curtis to network as well as Gordon Curtis! Quite the opposite is true, in fact—you'll adopt habits that are a better fit for you, improving your chances for success by personalizing your approach and developing a strategy that is right for you and that you're comfortable with. Once you understand your networking approach and have taken steps to strengthen it, you'll become much more confident as you contact others, and both the new approach and the new confidence will dramatically speed up the process of achieving your objectives.

And speaking of speeding things up: although both Joseph and Jane had spent months trying to achieve their objectives with not a single positive response, within a month after they began working with me, Joseph had gotten the funding he sought, and Jane was weighing three job offers—even though they needed to slow down (reassess) before they could come up to speed.

Stepping Back to Move Forward:
What Do You Need to Ask?

To understand your networking strategy and its potential unproductive and even negative consequences for achieving your goals, consider these four sets of questions regarding your own networking activity:

What's the goal?

- Why do you network?
- What do you hope to achieve with your current networking strategy?

Are you indulging in one-to-many broadsides?

- How often do you send out unsolicited articles, links, or other information to your network or post your social network profile or blog?
- How often do you forward e-mails you've received from other people to your network?

Are you spinning your wheels at events?

- How often do you attend meetings of professional associations, conferences, chambers of commerce, guilds, or other groups largely designed for networking?
- How many people whose business cards you have collected at such events do you actually circle back to, resulting in real mutual value?
- How much time do you spend in other face-to-face networking activities?
- How often have you walked out of one of these gatherings with bona fide leads, contacts, referrals, or other information that leads you directly to achieving a career or business goal?

How long does it all take?

- How much time do you actually spend networking?
- What percentage of your networking time is spent

    On social networking sites such as LinkedIn or Facebook?
    On the telephone?
    In face-to-face networking activities?

These are the questions I always raise with clients during initial meetings, so I can assess their current networking strengths and weaknesses. There's no one correct answer to any of them, but they help reveal patterns—in particular, spending significant amounts of time on activities that feel productive but in reality are generating little or no progress is a warning sign. These questions are designed to help you identify networking practices that you engage in out of habit but need to change in order to improve not just your rate of success but how quickly you're getting results. You probably find that many of the questions do not apply to your own networking approach, but insights generated by even one or two can make a huge difference.

The key is to make use of the whole range of resources—active as well as passive—proportionate to the results they yield, rather than focusing solely on electronic social networking. Social media makes it all too easy to be a gatherer, grazing on the array of connections that spreads out before you, and that's useful up to a point. But if that's all you're doing, you're missing out on the benefits of being a hunter as well—looking for particularly desirable connections that will take you directly to the results you want.

What's the Goal?

Why do you network? What do you hope to achieve with your current networking strategy?

If you have a coherent answer for these two questions, you're way ahead of the game, as they stump most of the people I ask. At any rate, although the people I work with have almost invariably come to me because they need to get results right away—having turned to me in desperation (way too late for comfort) because they have tried everything else they can think of—they rarely associate their networking activities with their current problems. Rather, they tend to describe their networking activities as part of a larger picture.

"I'm networking to build my network"—that's what the reply I get most often boils down to. For many people, networking has become an end in itself: the more Facebook friends, Twitter followers, or LinkedIn connections, the more success in the networking sweepstakes. Many of my clients describe this type of electronic armchair networking as "building their brand," which may well be true, but is not sufficient—if you do nothing else, the brand you build won't be nearly as productive for you as it might be.

Electronic armchair networking has become a fact of life, something almost everyone does, and many people simply don't question why they network at all. But when you define the purpose of networking in these terms, what follows is a false sense of security about what networking can do for you. Often, without knowing it, you assume that because you have such a large network you're protected in some way. It's not until an urgent and focused need arises that you discover the limits of your current networking strategy when people and information just aren't as accessible as your network numbers might suggest.

To assess the real value of your network, focus on this question: What do you have to show for your networking efforts to date? If you feel like you're spinning your wheels—you are.

Are You Indulging in One-to-Many Blasts?

How often do you send out unsolicited articles, links, or other information to your network? How often do you bulk-forward e-mails you've received from other people to your network?

If you engage in this type of activity even five times a year (and many people do it several times a week), you're at risk of contaminating your network—and damaging your image. Sending e-mail blasts is a classic example of networking in a random and unfocused way, and it's one of the actions you should avoid as you work to achieve your business or career objectives. Even if your business *is* direct mail, you need an element of focus. If you're not focused, and your message boils down to "don't forget about me," then you are at risk.

The first problem with this type of communication is that it's so impersonal. Impersonal communications have their place; people will happily read a well-designed marketing piece they've requested or a newsletter they've subscribed to, but that tolerance rarely extends to unsolicited secondhand e-mail. The sheer volume of e-mail most people receive makes it simply impossible to pay attention to the vast majority of messages. In addition, the more valuable the contact, the more likely the person is to be receiving a disproportionately high volume of e-mail. The same is true for purely self-serving posts to groups asking for "help."

To the great majority of your network contacts, this type of communication is just another nuisance e-mail or post to glance at and delete or ignore. You become identified as someone who doesn't take the time to get to know others and whose main purpose is to show up on the sender line of e-mails as often as possible. Each such communication can diminish or chip away at people's overall impression of you.

I'm not suggesting you should stop sending broadcast e-mail entirely. For instance, if you're moving to a new address or business location, or you're taking a new job or about to move to a new e-mail provider, you'll certainly want to let those in your network know. But there are very few other reasons to send e-mail blasts to your contacts for the purposes of personal networking. If you do have communications you're sure will appeal to a wide audience, use appropriate media—blog posts, comments on other people's posts, queries to mailing lists—and spare your personal network as much as you can.

Some in your network do appreciate sharing information through e-mail, and with them even forwarded messages can have a general positive effect in maintaining your network. But if you do forward links and other material and want a chance of having a positive impact, then you need to do it in a personalized way, addressing only the people in your network you know will appreciate what you're sending, and making it clear in each message that you're sending it to that specific recipient for a specific reason. This is one of the basic principles of the Right Person–Right Approach method: Do not network in a random and unfocused way. Instead, send personalized communications you know your contact will appreciate.

Are You Spinning Your Wheels at Events?

How often do you attend meetings of professional associations, conferences, chambers of commerce, guilds, or other groups largely designed for networking? How many people whose business cards you have collected at such events do you actually circle back to, resulting in real mutual value? How much time do you spend in other face-to-face networking activities? How often have you walked out of one of these gatherings with bona fide leads, contacts, referrals, or other information that leads you directly to achieving a career or business goal?

Don't get me wrong: I think it's a great idea to attend professional gatherings. But I've found that most people walk away from these get-togethers with a pocketful of business cards, a stiff neck from looking at other attendees' lapels, and the mistaken notion that they've engaged in an activity that will somehow improve their prospects in some way. If you're going to attend gatherings of this type, you must do so with specific goals in mind. Otherwise you're just reinforcing a bad habit.

The next time you attend a professional organization meeting or an organized networking event, instead of merely going through the motions, call the event's organizers and get a list of attendees. From that list, identify two or three people you'd like to meet, then do enough research on them to know why they would like to meet you—what you can offer to make it a mutually valuable connection and not merely a data dump in your favor. When you arrive, consult with the event coordinator and see whether they are willing to point out—or better still, introduce you to—the people you want to meet. That way you won't have to walk around staring at other people's name tags until you find the ones you'd like to talk with, and when you do find them, they will enjoy and remember the conversation as well as you do. You'll be surprised how receptive event coordinators will be to help you in this way. After all, they are likely staging the event largely for the purpose of stimulating productive networking exchange among attendees. As with all the activities in the Right Person–Right Approach method, you'll be networking with a laser focus and not simply doing the same thing over and over in the hope of getting different results.

How Long Does It All Take?

How much time do you spend networking? What percentage of your networking time is spent on social networking sites such as LinkedIn or Facebook? On the telephone? In face-to-face networking activities?

Although these questions have no right or wrong answer, there are consequences associated with spending too great a percentage of your time networking when that isn't what you're being paid for. If you're networking in a random and unfocused way, contaminating your network with unwanted and impersonal communications, and repeating techniques that rarely generate results for you, you're wasting effort and reducing your chances of success. And if you're spending significant amounts of time in this type of activity, you're taking time away from what could be much more productive networking activities.

Begin right now to change your networking strategy. For starters, eliminate random, impersonal, and unfocused communications. For example, before you offer to connect with someone on LinkedIn, think about what you have to offer that person beyond another node for their personal network. Rather than leaving the generic invitation text in place, say something like this: "Dear Joe, You have come to mind regarding some recent research I'm doing on XYZ. I'd like to invite you to join my LinkedIn network in hopes that we might be able to share notes on this subject." Don't allow yourself to be lulled into the false sense of security that just "being out there" and blithely connecting with hundreds, even thousands, of people can bring. Begin to think in terms of targeted networking activity, whether electronic or in person.

What you need to do is be more than a gatherer—strolling along and snacking on roots and berries as they appear—but think like a hunter as well; that is, identify your target and go after it the way a hunter goes after game.

This is one of my favorite analogies: the two basic survival strategies—gathering and hunting—are as much a factor in business as in a tide pool. All across the range of living creatures, some collect what they need from their environment as they drift past it or it drifts past them, while others go out looking for what they need and chase it down if it isn't just sitting there. Still others do both, and they tend to be the most successful of all. Even if you're not faced with a situation in which you must produce immediate results, cultivating a combined approach will refine your networking skills in ways that will pay significant dividends as you move forward.

Once again, this doesn't mean trying to change who you are—just what you do. Examine your networking strategy and refocus it. Modify your networking habits by introducing sounder practices from the Right Person–Right Approach method, and that will enable you to achieve the success you seek.

What Are You Communicating?

Once you've examined your networking strategy, the next step is to identify the message you're sending out with your communications to your network. Although determining the extent to which you send impersonal and random messages to your network is part of this, you also need to examine the content of the communications you write personally.

For example, consider the e-mail message in the box below. You've probably gotten notes like this one, and maybe you've sent a few yourself—I know I get variations on the same theme all the time. Many people broadcast messages like it to dozens if not hundreds of their acquaintances and associates when they need something:

Hi, [NameFilledInByMergeProgram],

Hope this note finds you well. My position at MCL was eliminated last week. Although caught a bit off guard, I remain optimistic about some developing opportunities.

I expect to be doing some leadership and strategy work at the Reed Institute in Chattanooga over the next

(Continued)

months. However, my priority remains to find another full-time role in the HR Leadership area in an organization ripe for innovation and change. Previously, I was limited by my inability to relocate, and that has now changed.

Anyway, I wanted to briefly reach out to some friends and associates to advise of my status change, and to request that you forward any opportunities that may cross your path. Have attached a current résumé for your consideration and feedback.

Best Regards,
Geri

The sender has made several errors that even reasonably successful networkers still make in many different forms of written and verbal communications. First, the focus is on the sender. After a perfunctory "Hope this finds you well," it goes on to explain what's going on in the sender's life—the loss of a job, some of the activities she'll be engaging in over the next few months, the fact that she's now able to relocate. To be effective, any communication you send out must focus on the person you're communicating with—not on you. And that is impossible to do en masse.

Next, it's impersonal. Because Geri uses the blandest of general terms—things she could say to anyone, with none of the details that would catch a specific reader's attention—those receiving it will almost certainly feel on some level that they're being lumped in with a group and that no effort has been made to treat them as individuals. If you want real help from the recipients, design communications such as this for the purpose of establishing a value-based relationship. Geri could have at least indicated that she would be more than happy to share her campaign findings about the industry with those interested and willing to compare notes and exchange leads. It's worth repeating: such communications simply must be personal and can never be broadcast to a group of people.

Third, it's not at all clear what Geri wants. She indicates she's looking for a position in "HR Leadership," and she's attached a résumé, but the recipients are left to guess whether she wants them to pass it on or read it carefully and recommend changes that would make it more effective. At best, readers are likely to ask themselves whether they know of any HR leadership positions up for grabs—and will answer "Nope!" and skip to the next message. But if Geri had asked whether they knew of anyone they could suggest she speak to in HR leadership (getting her closer to her goal), then she'd be posing a question many could answer yes to. If you want something of the person you're communicating with, you not only need to make it clear what you're asking for, but you also need to frame the question in the right terms.

If you frame your message properly, based on your research into the recipient's needs and challenges as they relate to your proposition, you can spark enough interest that attaching a document—résumé, business plan, proposal, or whatever—isn't even necessary. The key is to arouse interest and prompt questions rather than answer them. Once someone expresses interest, you have the opportunity to inquire more specifically about the person's needs, challenges, situation, or whatever issues your proposition can be tailored to address. Armed with that information, you then can confidently send the *right* supporting material, or links to it, highlighting the aspects you now know are most transferable or relevant.

The next example is based on an e-mail message that I crafted with one of my clients that illustrates how this can work. (It was even stronger in the original, which named names at every point, but I've glossed over the details here to preserve privacy.)

To: {Specific Individual}

Subject: A thank-you, a request, and an offer.

[Firstname],

Thank you for the invitation to tomorrow's webinar. I'm looking forward to your company's perspective and insights, as I'm currently leading an effort to incorporate social media into my company's demand-generation campaigns.

I am researching a variety of opportunities, and not surprisingly, my target companies, like yours, are those implementing "best-in-class" marketing automation.

I can't help but think I could easily keep an eye out for opportunities for you. And it goes without saying that I would greatly value your insight in identifying organizations that meet our joint criteria, as well as your input regarding my campaign.

Would you be open to a conversation further exploring such mutual interests? With a better understanding of your qualified client criteria and prospect companies, I'm sure I could be a source of leads—including new opportunities within the company that's acquiring mine. I'm also happy to share findings from our recent social media activities and the deployment of our in-house system.

If it's convenient for you, I'm available to meet in the upcoming weeks before the new year. I'll give you a call to follow up, or, if you'd prefer that I speak with your admin to set a time, please e-mail me contact info.

Best Regards,
[Full Name of Sender]

In contrast, Geri's message makes her sound like someone who's at loose ends: she's going to take some time to do some work in her area, and she'd like readers to get back to her if they hear of anything. It's a classic example of a communication likely to make a negative impression on those it's sent to, not to mention that it's highly unlikely to yield any positive results. Nonetheless, I see people send such hopeful but doomed communications all the time.

What's Your Message?

To get a handle on what you're communicating, collect a sample of networking-specific messages you've sent recently in an effort to get something from others. Select messages addressed to individuals or to your network for the purpose of accomplishing a specific objective, such as gathering industry, benchmark, trend, market, competitive, or global information or research data; asking for help with a job search; looking for a referral; or getting a recommendation. E-mail messages may be the easiest to find, but also consider your posts to discussion groups and invitations to join you on a social networking site. Your sample can be as few as three or four messages or as many as fifteen or twenty.

Make notes for each message that answer these questions:

- Is your communication personal? Do you ask specific questions about how the recipient is doing in matters of interest to that person? Or is it sent to a group of people in your network without being a newsletter they've requested?

- Is the focus of the e-mail *you* and *your* needs? Or do you also focus on your recipient and what that person might need?

- Do you clearly state what you're asking for? And are you asking for it in a way people can answer easily?

- If you're seeking information, do you explain why you need it?

- Is there any inherent value to the reader?

- Is there any potential benefit to the reader if they respond with what you are asking of them?

Answering these questions will begin to give you a sense of the message that you're sending out in various communications. As you go forward with the Right Person–Right Approach method, this will be another of the foundation blocks you build on.

Does this seem like too much work? Give it a chance; it may seem like more work at first, but in the end you're likely to find that it's so easy compared to the results you get that it feels almost like cheating. As one of my clients told me, "I hope you use these powers only for good." For better or for worse, we are all evaluated by the messages we send, even the most superficial. Everything you say will influence your audience's perceptions—so if you know how, you can manage them to your benefit.

Who Is Your Audience?

In addition to communicating the right message, you need to communicate to the right people. Geri made the mistake of reaching out indiscriminately to anyone and everyone in her network—broadcasting blindly, with no attempt to screen out the people who might not be able to help her, and no attempt to personalize her e-mail. And how could she, with so many recipients? It's a classic example of the "more is better" mistake that so many people make when they're initiating the pursuit of a career or business objective.

But that's not the only mistake you need to avoid. It does no good to refine your list if you focus it on the wrong people. And surprisingly enough, the wrong people may be the ones who could decide to give you your job or your money or whatever your present end goal is. They'll be the right people later, after you've done your research, but you can't give them a reason to listen to you yet. Hold off on approaching decision makers at this stage of the process—the M&A person who would review your business plan and determine whether to buy your company, the department head or HR director who would decide whether or not you get the job, the guru who would decide whether to give you the information you're seeking. Addressing such targets too soon is as dangerous as casting your net too wide. You might scrounge up something that way, but it's more likely that you'll simply waste their time—and yours. Until you have the perfect business plan, proposal, résumé, or whatever—one that will stand out among the hundreds vying for their attention—they have no reason to talk to you. Instead of casting your net too wide, you're casting it too soon and missing the fish.

Joseph and Jane were making that mistake: they were targeting decision makers too early in the process. When Joseph managed to secure a meeting or a phone call, he immediately launched into his sales pitch. To each of the decision makers he contacted, he explained his company's products, his financial needs, and the expected return on investment he felt certain he could deliver. He knew that venture capital firms were his primary sources, but he didn't accept that he needed to do more groundwork before he was ready to meet with them. Like so many, he was driven to just get out there and make it happen. It is really hard to take the time to do this work, especially if other stakeholders in your success (bosses, significant others) are measuring you based on activity like numbers of calls, résumés sent, pitches, doors knocked on, and the like. Nonetheless, you need to do what any world-class sales organization does: define the market, research the market, and package the product, and only then target the market. Anything else is just activity. Despite Joseph's outgoing personality and his enthusiasm for his company and its products—the positives on which his networking strategy was built—he had wasted nearly six months contacting decision makers, and it wasn't until he paused to do some research that he began to get results.

Although Jane had a very different personality from Joseph's, she was also making the mistake of reaching out directly and prematurely to decision makers, in this case HR directors. Her success record was identical to Joseph's—zilch—but she thought she was being productive. When asked how her progress was going, her answer was always something like this: "It's good—I have tons of résumés out there and I'm talking to everyone—lots of good *activity*."

So if it isn't safe to broadcast to the world or to target decision makers, who's left? Although your intermediate goal in your search is to find the critical enabler—the one person best able to arm you with the information and introduction you need to tip a decision maker in your favor—even a potential critical enabler may be unable to help you if what you are asking of them is unclear or if they just don't have a good enough reason to want to help you. It's best to practice with lower-stakes contacts first, not only for their feedback on your focus and clarity of request but also for the sounding-board effect—to hear yourself talk. Like any pitch, it takes practice to present this one smoothly, authentically, and compellingly. Thus your very first round of communications should go to trusted advisers—people likely to know the general outlines of your objectives, and to be both well-disposed toward you and willing to provide critical feedback; help you test and refine your inquiry; and, with luck, give you enough information to help you identify a critical enabler and prepare a proposal that will engage that person's interest.

One of the most important reasons for testing with trusted advisers is to solicit their feedback, getting them to play devil's advocate and poke holes in your objective and request. If people who are in a position to provide substantial direct help—to act as decision makers or critical enablers—don't understand what exactly you are asking of them, they are very unlikely to provide feedback as to their reaction. Instead, they'll just give you the standard brush-off responses: "I'll keep an eye out for you" or "I'll let you know if I come up with anything."

Hence the trusted-adviser step serves as a critical check in the process to ensure that you are asking for something that makes sense. Although this step may seem overly simple and even feel like a waste of time, it can save you months. Every day, I get requests like "Let me know if you know of a good search firm or distribution partner"— and I simply don't know how to help. It's frustrating; I know I could help, and it is my nature to want to help, but I just don't have enough to go on and don't have the time to seek clarity about the real question.

Who's Your Target?

To see if you're reaching out to the wrong people or even the right people prematurely, do another type of analysis of your messaging, e-mail, telephone, and face-to-face communications. List one or more career or business objectives you've pursued in the past year or so. These can include smaller objectives, such as trying to get one of your policy recommendations considered by a department head, or more significant ones, such as trying to gain a promotion or trying to get funding for your company.

Once you've listed your business objectives, think about the communications you've sent in support of each of those objectives. Look through your sent-messages files, your e-mail address book, or other records to identify the patterns. Ask yourself these questions:

1. What proportion of the messages in pursuit of this objective went to a group of people with minimal personalization?

2. Of the messages that were written for specific individuals, what proportion went to each of the following groups:

   Trusted advisers (people who could answer fairly general but specific questions about the topic)?
   Critical enablers (people who could provide detailed knowledge and introductions to the gatekeepers for your objective)?
   Decision makers (people in your ultimate audience, who were in the position to buy, approve, fund, or sponsor your objective)?

Now consider your results. Did you get a reply at all? Did you get what you wanted?

If you sense that you've been targeting the wrong people (or even the right people in the wrong way or at the wrong time) and don't feel you need detailed proof of this, you can simply ponder the effects of your communications. When was the last time someone really helped you out in a way that you would consider a significant advance toward your objectives? OK, so when did someone help you just a little bit based on a specific inquiry you made?

It turns out that people who approach decision makers directly early in the process of pursuing a career or business objective have success rates little better than those of people who rely on generic broadsides. This is another way of contaminating a network. Why? Decision makers have to control their time especially closely, and if they don't have a reason to respond to a message, they won't do it—but they will remember the attempt, at least well enough to put your name in the don't-bother category. This means your first task is to find the people who will get you to the decision makers in terms that are useful and impressive to them.

How Successful Have You Been?

Most of my clients come to me after they've tried conventional approaches to achieving business objectives. In other words, they've taken the route I took when I was first trying to get into outplacement, and they've broadcast requests to their networks and contacted as many people as they can, telling them what they need. Even those who submit résumés to HR or post them on job-search Web sites are still trying to reach as many people as they can. They reason that even if they get only one positive response out of hundreds, they've succeeded in what they were trying to do. But they just don't understand the odds—and the odds are against them.

Among the problems with this approach is that it's very inefficient. For instance, if you send out an e-mail blast to five hundred people in your network, and one of them replies with useful information, your success ratio is a minuscule two tenths of one percent. And if you come away from a professional organization meeting with forty business cards, how many of them can you count as resulting in a positive outcome? In most cases, the answer will be zero. Even if you do get a positive outcome from one or two of the contacts from random networking such as this, the success ratio is still very low relative to the time and effort expended.

Beyond inefficiency, this approach is downright dangerous. That one lead realized from the five-hundred-address blast comes at the cost of antagonizing some or all of the other 99.98 percent of the list. Unless the current objective is the only one you'll ever have, be wary of reducing your chances of achieving future objectives still further.

The Right Person–Right Approach standard for measuring results is the exact opposite of this. It's all about being efficient and targeted with your communications— and achieving very high success rates. In fact, in almost every case the ratio of networking-related communications initiated by my clients to useful responses received is virtually one-to-one. I define a "useful response" as a referral, or information that can be used to advance the seeker's objective, or the achievement of the objective itself—but *not* a general pat on the head. No matter how pumped up you feel when someone says you're brilliant, it does you no good unless the person also offers to do something for you or tell you something you need to know. The Right Person–Right Approach method is the most efficient way to advance and achieve your career and business objectives, virtually guaranteeing you a 100-percent success rate. And achieving that high success rate is what you should set your sights on.

Are You Hitting Your Target?

To see how you're doing, review your communications once more, this time to determine how successful you've been. Again, if you don't feel the need to do this exercise in great detail, you can simply review your communications generally to get a sense of your success rate. If you asked the person you wrote to for what you wanted from them, did you get it? Or, are you reaching out to others for help at all?

To perform a more detailed analysis of how successful you've been, do the following: Assuming you've saved your e-mails in an organized way, look back through them for the responses you've received. Make a list of your phone calls and in-person meetings as well.

Once you've gathered your initial communications together and counted the total number you've made, analyze the effectiveness of your overtures to determine your hit rate. To do that, divide the number of people you reached out to by the number of people who responded to your initial approach. This represents your hit rate. For instance, if you reached out to fifty-five people in order to get information about a specific subject, and six responded, your hit rate would be six in fifty-five, or about 11 percent. Typically, when they first come into my office, my clients have hit rates ranging from one in fifty to one in one hundred or more. That is, for every fifty to one hundred e-mails or social networking messages they send out or phone calls they make, they get one positive response. Or, they aren't reaching out for help at all.

Once you've determined your hit rate, identify what the take-away was from each of your hits. A take-away in this case is an "advance"—a clear positive response from a contact in the form of a lead or a referral or usable bit of intelligence, information that advances your pursuit of your objective.

Use the following categories to sort your approaches and assess your rate of success. Make a separate chart for each method of contact in the Description category.

Description: Type of contact—e-mail, phone, meeting, or whatever

  #: Number of people for each description

  Result: Number of useful responses

  Type of Useful Response:

Satisfaction of objective

Referral

Lead or other usable intelligence

Your aim should be to achieve a one-to-one hit ratio: every contact you make should produce solid information that advances your business objective. If you're not meeting with success virtually every time you reach out to someone, you're wasting time—yours and that of the people you reach out to—and in the bargain you may be contaminating your network, interrupting people who may see your communications as intrusive or unwanted.

What's the Bottom Line?

I'm speaking from experience here. When I take clients through the type of networking strategy analysis presented in this chapter, it's a pleasure to see the light bulb go on as they begin to understand the negative consequences— from wasting time to damaging their brand to contaminating their networks—that some of their networking practices can cause. I tell them not to beat themselves up—and that's good advice for you, too. It's unlikely that you could have become aware of these ill effects on your own. In addition, it's likely that any damage you've done can be undone over time using the Right Person–Right Approach method.

People who move further along with the Right Person– Right Approach method always find that worry over lack of results diminishes and disappears, and confidence replaces it. Where they'd been shooting from the hip, working without a plan, they learn that they can preserve and manage their networks in a targeted and meaningful way and can use their networks efficiently, effectively, and purposefully. This allows them to add value in the process—cultivating their networks without depleting them. They can be successful, despite past frustrations, because they have a detailed strategy to follow.

If you've gone through the suggested self-assessment and analysis to examine your networking strategy, you've probably discovered some obstacles to your achieving your business and career objectives. That's progress—if you can't see an obstacle, it's hard to remove it.

Understanding the flaws in your current networking strategy through analyzing what, how, and to whom you're communicating is the foundation for the Right Person-Right Approach method. Although it might initially appear that its focus is somewhat negative, it's important that you understand just how much time and effort you're using up without receiving a return. Then you can redirect your networking communications to make them more effective and efficient, and you can begin achieving positive results.

CHAPTER 3

Articulating Your Objective

"I gotta grow," George told me when he walked into my office.

George is the founder and owner of a seven-year-old business with annual gross sales in the $750,000 range. The company specializes in creating high-end custom architectural wood products, and other elements used in home construction and remodeling. He sells directly to end users, and he also sells to construction companies and through architects. At the time we met, he'd expanded from the New England region, where his offices and manufacturing facility are located, to reach customers up and down the East Coast. But he felt he'd hit a plateau, and his business seemed stalled.

One of the primary reasons George, like so many people, was having difficulty achieving his objective was that he'd not articulated it clearly. In fact, he hadn't really figured out what he was after at all beyond a very general notion of his goal: to grow. His inability to state clearly what he was trying to accomplish was holding him back. The "act first, articulate later" approach very rarely achieves optimal results, even when the results appear to be positive. You need to make sure you can describe how you want to achieve the outcome you want, and that means that you must articulate your objective very precisely.

I asked him to clarify what he meant when he talked about "growing," because to me there are a hundred different ways to grow:

"Do you need to add more products? Expand your facility? Hire additional workers? What is it exactly that you have to do in order to grow?"

"Well, I need to hire someone," George responded. "Or I need to find a partner, and I need funding in order to do that . . . and so I'm asking everyone I bump into whether they know of anybody who'd be interested in investing in a company like mine."

He felt he wasn't at the stage where he could engage a business broker, and being a staunchly independent New Englander, he figured he would just go it alone, despite feeling stalled. In other words, although George had a general vision of where he wanted to be when he'd reached his goal, he didn't have a clear idea of what he needed to do to get there.

Like many entrepreneurs, George was so immersed in running his business that the thought of approaching either investors or partners, or even of searching for the right employee who might help him grow his business, was overwhelming. A classic business Catch-22. The result was that he had been reduced to reaching out in a very disorganized, sporadic, and unfocused way. He was so busy working in the business that he wasn't able to step back and work on the business. He'd only been able to articulate his needs to the point where he was pretty sure he knew he needed money or help or both. Even though he had an uneasy feeling that he was going about it in the wrong way, he still felt compelled to be doing something.

George's dilemma illustrates one of the most important things you need to do when you frame your objectives: you need to state them in a very clear way—remembering that *clear* is in the eyes of the beholder. And the measure of that clarity is the extent to which people can really help you. But first you must define your objective to the point that it leads you to those right people—the people who have the information and the contacts you need in order to achieve the outcome you desire.

So What *Is* Your Objective?

Approaching friends and business associates for help in achieving poorly articulated objectives and business goals is one of the main sources of unproductive networking, on a par with the e-mail blasts discussed in Chapter Two. When you ask someone to help you find something as general as "consulting opportunities," for instance, you're invariably going to get the business equivalent of a blank stare: "I'll be in touch if I hear of anything." You'll discover the reason when you do an Internet search on that statement and find that you get upward of a million hits. No one walks around with such a vast amount of information in the search engine between their ears.

By articulating your objectives in a systematic way, you'll also narrow them down. In this case, more is not merrier. Instead, less—in the sense of "narrower"—is apt to be better when it comes to articulating objectives. Although it's possible to be too specific—to look only for jobs for left-handed pastry cooks—most people find they need to narrow down their objectives rather than broaden them as they seek to achieve any business or career goal.

The biggest problem I see is the tendency to be wary of narrowing down objectives. There is a deep fear that if you are too specific you will miss out on the world of opportunities, funding, clients, employees. George was a classic example of that. His reasoning went something like this: "If I keep my criteria very general, I'm going to be exposed to a lot more people than if I narrow them down, and the more people I'm exposed to, the more likely it is that good things will happen." He was afraid to be too specific for fear that a detailed list of criteria would result in his coming up with nothing.

The problem with this line of reasoning is that if you adopt the more-is-better approach, you'll wind up talking with dozens, even hundreds of dead-end contacts before you find the right one—if you ever do. If, for instance, you're simply looking for "investors," you could spend the rest of your business career sifting through thousands of potential matches and never come up with the right one. Expressing your objective in very general terms is grossly inefficient. It is both easy and dangerous to fall prey to the "I'll know it when I see it" rationale for your reluctance to spell out a goal.

Without losing sight of your ultimate goal, you need to put it aside temporarily for the purpose of identifying the steps that will take you where you want to go. That's what articulating your objective is all about. Although George was worried that he would be looking for a needle in a haystack, the fact is that the past ten years or so have seen the development of many powerful tools for finding precisely the sort of needles he wanted. I call them "intersections," because you find them by discovering where your specific needs intersect with those of the customers and clients you're seeking, or the people who make it their business to know exactly what you're looking for, or who can provide the service or job or information you need.

Like Joseph and Jane in Chapter Two, many of my clients argue that my approach feels too indirect. They really want to go straight to the people who could make the decision to help them—the venture capitalist with money looking for a home or the HR director with jobs to fill. Nonetheless, in the pursuit of a business objective, the direct approach is almost always the long way around; the indirect approach really is the most efficient way to achieve your business objectives. That's true well beyond business, after all. Migrating fish, for example, often go great distances out of their way to benefit from the Gulf Stream. Once there, they are whisked toward their destination in a fraction of the time it would have taken them if they had swum directly.

George was able to accomplish in a single week an objective that he had been pursuing for over a year—one that, had he continued on the path he was on, would easily have taken him years more and might have proved completely out of reach. The secret to George's success lies in the following pages.

How Do You Refine Your Objectives?

Objectives come in two flavors: macro and micro. Your macro objective is the initial statement of your desired outcome. A *macro objective* is a starting point, a broad statement of where you want to be or what you want to achieve. If you're an entrepreneur, your macro objective might be something like "I see my company with as many as twenty-five new employees occupying a new manufacturing facility that will enable us to broaden our market beyond the five-state region we currently serve." If you're searching for a job, your macro objective might be "I see myself working for a corporation or a unit that specializes in market research." And if you're looking to increase sales, your macro objective might be "I want to meet my personal goal of selling $150 million worth of my company's product line in the coming year."

In other words, stating your macro objective means envisioning what you want to achieve and putting it into words. But it's more than that: even if your macro objective is something as general as George's "I gotta grow," it's your starting point. Using the Right Person–Right Approach method, once you've stated your macro objective, you break that statement down into a series of smaller components, or *micro objectives*. They represent the individual legs of the trip that will take you most efficiently and effectively and quickly to your objective.

I call this process of articulating your objective one of developing "extreme clarity." It begins with your vision of what you're aiming for, then it enables you to find the path to that target. Each of the micro objectives into which you break down your macro objective must be characterized by having a direct impact on its achievability.

How Do You Measure the Accuracy of an Objective Statement?

As you articulate your objective, you need to find a way to measure its success in order to determine how well you've articulated it, how understandable each of the micro objectives is. You do that by consulting a trusted adviser, someone you can go to when you need to know whether you're articulating your objective in a way that is easy to understand. Your trusted adviser will often be a good friend or associate—someone you work with or do business with—because you need someone who knows you well, someone who will give you a direct and honest answer, who will tell you if you're not explaining your objective in a way that people will understand. It helps to have a trusted adviser who knows the particular market or industry or specialization you're trying to penetrate, but the most important thing is to find someone willing to think critically and not politely about the ideas or inquiry you are testing. Candid feedback is hard to come by and needs to be solicited accordingly, even as you avoid the temptation to seek out and heed feedback from those who will tell you what you want to hear.

But in addition to friends and associates, there's another very reliable adviser you can consult. The Internet can be hugely powerful when you're trying to find out whether the terms you're using to describe your objectives are narrowed down enough to be manageable. Unlike most human advisers, the Internet is unflinchingly honest—sometimes painfully so. It is so honest that it will tell you the exact number of hits you are getting and the difference in those hits that a single word added, subtracted, or changed can make. The Internet is the perfect tool for determining whether the words you're using as you articulate your objective are too general. And its patience is infinite—which cannot be said for even your closest friends—so it's a good idea to use it first, before turning to your trusted human advisers.

Most people's initial statements of their objectives have one thing in common: they're far too general for someone to know exactly how to help. When you're working with a trusted adviser—whether it's a business associate, a friend, or the Internet—you're essentially doing a keyword search, and one of the first things you need to do is refine your keywords. Consider how George put this to work for him.

Real-Life Challenge: Escaping Generalities

For George, the Internet proved to be precisely the trusted adviser he was looking for. When we began to break down his macro objective ("I gotta grow") into micro objectives, it became clear that raising capital was one of the things he felt he needed to do. In this case, we wrote down, as one of the micro objectives into which we were breaking down George's macro objective, the keyword "investors."

We discovered the obvious when we did an Internet search on that word: it produced millions of options. George still had a long way to go before he'd articulated his objective well enough to be able to put a fruitful search into motion. The fact that the search keyword "investors" barely narrowed down his choices at all pinpointed for George why he hadn't been able to move forward with his growth initiative. He was trying to chase down a funding source or a partner randomly, approaching investors one by one. What he needed to do instead was to find a way to refine the field of investors so he could find a meaningful way to approach them. That was the only way he'd be able to find the path to his objective of growing his business.

We further articulated George's search by adding terms that represented micro objectives. Our next step was a geographical narrowing: we limited our search to investors who were located in the "New England" region. We also determined that he needed someone who understood his business, so we further narrowed the search with the phrase "quality home products." We also determined that it would be helpful if George's investor knew the primary area of expansion he perceived in his market, so we added "network of architects" to our list of terms. And finally, because we were looking for someone with experience building businesses like George's, we added "scale a small business."

The word *services* can mean many things when you're articulating your objective, but it's still useful when combined with enough other qualifiers. George and I added the word "services" to our search string to help locate people who sold to the group we wanted to approach, or who wrote about them, or had done research or analysis on their business—in short, anyone who might have accumulated knowledge of and been acquainted personally with the investors we were looking to attract.

George now had a much firmer grasp of what he needed to do to reach his goal. He understood that he was looking for an investor or venture capital firm that served small businesses selling into the home products market through architects in the New England region. Once we'd articulated his macro objective by adding specific keywords, or micro objectives, George performed an Internet search. His search turned up the Institute for Family-Owned Business (www.fambusiness.org)—a company that specialized in finding partners and investors for precisely the kind of small business George had built. The president of the organization was the perfect fit for George, and within a week after the two first talked, he had connected George with the investor and business partner he was looking for, the retired owner of a custom furniture business who was looking for precisely the kind of company George had developed in order to help it do what he himself had done in the past: scale a small business.

What's *Your* Objective?

To articulate your own business or career objective, follow these steps:

1. Write down one important career or business objective you'd like to achieve in the near future. Your first attempt at a macro objective can be very general, along the lines of "get promoted to district sales manager" or "increase my personal sales and the sales in my district by 15 percent" or "get funding to expand my manufacturing facility" or "obtain information that will enable me to complete a

report to my vice president on the feasibility of the new sales strategy."

2. Begin to break down your objective by identifying at least five micro objectives in the form of keywords you can use in an Internet search to determine that you've narrowed down your search sufficiently. These terms should put limits on your search. If, for instance, you need to limit your search to your specific geographic area, you should include the name of your city, state, or region, as appropriate. If you're looking for investors, that term should be part of your search. If your search is industry specific, that's another important keyword. The list of micro objectives can also include terms from the following categories:

- Product or service

- Market segment

- Type of business

It is a common mistake to use language that is subject to definition by a search engine or a person. Hence, the key is to use objective nouns such as "insurance," "innovation," or "growth" and avoid subjective adjectives such as "successful," "innovative," or "growing."

3. Search the Internet. As you're adding keywords that represent your micro objectives to your search string, consider trying different search engines: Google, Bing, Yahoo, and so on. The more key words, the better. I've found some of the most effective search strings to be up to fifteen words. It's instructive to begin with an initial search

term, one that best describes your macro objective. Keep a list of the keyword search strings and the number of hits generated by each. Save the search results, or write down how many hits you receive with each search. Early in the process, this number will generally be in the hundreds of thousands, even millions.

4. Compile a list of "targets." Continue to refine your search by adding micro objectives or changing the ones you have until you generate a list of targets—organizations, sources of information, or decision makers—to which you need to gain access to achieve your objective. For example, if your macro objective is to "find a job in clean tech," searching on that string will generate a very large list of targets. When you add micro objectives such as "wind power" and "South Carolina" to designate the specific sector and geographic location you're looking for, your list of targets will be significantly smaller. In most cases, you should add micro objectives to your search string until the number of hits generated is less than one thousand.

Have fun with your search! Experimenting with long search strings can be like a treasure hunt. It also will help you think, "What keywords have I been sharing in my networking attempts to date? Are any of the words that make sense to me likely to be throwing people off?" Here is one example of this kind of keyword trap: a client learned from this process that he actually had been confusing his audience by using the acronym CRM and the term "Web 2.0." He thought he knew exactly what these meant—but when he tested the terms with trusted advisers, he discovered that they all thought *they* knew, too—but each adviser had a different definition.

Real-Life Challenge: Articulating Your Objectives

The following stories demonstrate how the process works when applied to three common objectives: business development, job search, and information gathering. The goal in each case is to get to a *real*, substantive response instead of one of the common polite brush-offs. It's all too easy to take comfort from statements like "What you are doing and asking for is really interesting, and I'll definitely call you if I hear of that" or unqualified, weak, or obvious leads like "Have you checked out Monster.com?" When you follow the Right Person–Right Approach method, you don't need to let this sort of lame and uncomfortable attempt to help satisfy you.

Business Development: Separate Searches, Multiple Results

Tim's consulting practice consisted of applying methods he'd learned to streamline manufacturing processes to other types of businesses, including insurance and financial services. Tim described himself as a "good networker," someone who had a lot of contacts and who had been asking "everyone" whether they could help him find new "operations consulting opportunities." He was seeking to increase sales for his business by developing new clients, but he'd been hitting the wall when he asked his friends and business associates to help him.

The key reason Tim wasn't able to get any help from his friends was that he was presenting a very high-level macro objective with his statement. In fact, when we plugged the words "operations consulting opportunities" into our search engine, we got back a million and a half hits. The key for Tim was to refine his objective so that he could find the path to his stated goal.

We began by adding micro objectives that would narrow Tim's search down to a useful point. We started by specifying his geographical area, Philadelphia, and by specifying the business sectors he wanted to target, insurance and financial services companies. Tim's situation was interesting because it involved a search for what I call "hidden gems." We were developing micro objectives that identified external manifestations of hidden internal needs or problems. It's very easy to identify the major players—the large insurance and financial services companies that are well established and whose names everyone knows. The key for Tim was to find the smaller, less established companies—the ones that might need his services.

To do that, we asked ourselves, "What external, visible characteristics can we look for that are symptoms that a company might have problems that you know how to solve?" It's a question that everyone seeking to increase sales or expand a business needs to ask. In its more general form, it can be stated as "What problems do your product or service solve?" and "How do you identify companies that have those problems so that you can sell your products or services to them?" These questions evoked a number of useful search terms:

Rapid growth: Companies that have recently experienced dramatic growth typically struggle to update their IT systems, which generally haven't been developed with a scalable infrastructure.

Regulatory problems: Companies that have recently run into trouble with regulatory agencies for questionable practices under such regulations as Sarbanes-Oxley often look to IT improvements to keep them out of trouble, but they lack the internal talent to produce what they need.

Enterprise software conversion: Companies that have recently undergone enterprise-wide software conversion— from SAP to PeopleSoft, for instance—typically encounter a host of issues of the kind Tim was expert at dealing with.

Mergers: Companies emerging from recent mergers or acquisitions generally need to consolidate and integrate systems—and therefore need someone to figure out how to streamline and integrate new and complex processes.

Lower revenues: Companies whose revenues have been shrinking but have been unable to raise prices to compensate for reduced income often need to implement systems changes to increase efficiency and lower costs.

At first Tim was frustrated that we seemed to be taking a circuitous route to his objective, but he finally saw that each of these micro objectives enabled him to move closer to articulating his objective in a way that would lead him toward achieving it. His question had become, "What insurance or financial services companies can we identify that are experiencing one or more of these conditions?" We searched each of these categories individually at first, combining his initial limiters with "rapid growth," then with "regulatory problems," then with "mergers," then with "systems integration," then with "lower revenues." This produced five separate lists, each of which provided between ten and twenty companies that might well need Tim's services and that were the best prospects for his continuing research.

Job Search: Avoiding Subjective Language

Dylan was a brilliant IT specialist who had held jobs in many industries and who, by his own description, specialized in radical and innovative technical solutions for highly complex situations. His experience was so diverse that, as he put it, "My résumé transcends definition." That was one of his problems, which most of my clients share. Another problem could be found in the statement of his macro objective: to find "a really cool entrepreneurial company thinking outside the box with a really interesting product for which I can help build the Web interface and for which I can help develop the social networking and marketing approach." Another of the words that emerged as we tossed his macro objective around was "disruptive."

He was looking for a company that was poised to "disrupt" an industry with a new, paradigm-changing product. He perceived himself as an innovator, a disruptor, and he'd been presenting himself as that to everyone he talked with as he conducted his job search, but to no avail.

Now although Dylan is clearly not your garden-variety IT specialist, even given his somewhat flamboyant way of describing himself, the problem was not with the dictionary definitions of the specific words he used in his macro objective. The problem was, they were all very abstract and each would likely be defined in a highly subjective way by the people who heard them. The keywords in his macro were open to wildly varying interpretations—not to mention creating revulsion in response to so many overused buzzwords! There was no way he could obtain any objective, measurable results using his current statement, especially when he asked his friends and associates for help.

When we began to examine the meanings of some of the words he used, he explained the term *disruptive* by identifying examples of products, technologies, and practices that had changed entire industries as they were introduced and emerged. These included such obvious phenomena as the iPhone, nanotechnology, and social networking. In addition, Dylan loved pretty much any vehicle that was powered by an internal combustion engine. The problem was that he didn't want to work for a company that had already introduced such market disruptors fifty years ago; he wanted to work for a leading-edge company that was *in the midst of* introducing products or technologies like these. So the question for Dylan became, "How do you identify companies that are ready to introduce radical, disruptive, paradigm-changing products into an existing industry but have not yet done so?"

We began to narrow his search by introducing keywords that were fairly easy to identify. He didn't want to move, so we used "Atlanta," his home city, as one of our keywords. He knew that he didn't want to work for a large company, so we introduced the term "start-up." He couldn't afford to work for equity, so he needed to find a company with a proven concept that had secured significant funding and could pay him a salary. He was also taken with devices; he wanted to work for a company that was developing a technology-based device or product or an innovative way to develop and market an existing product with high *disruptive potential*. We'd gotten as far as "venture-funded companies, Atlanta, disruptive technologies."

Dylan played with various search strings including these variables and others, including products such as airplanes, automobiles, boats, and other types of vehicles. He spent several days, on and off, refining his search strings and introducing new variables, until his search produced a very interesting result: an Atlanta-based automobile manufacturer whose business was redefining the automotive manufacturing industry by producing semi-custom cars that clients could design and order over the Internet. Dylan had found the match he was looking for: a company whose "disruptive" profile fit exactly with what he perceived to be his own capabilities and interests.

Information-Gathering: Helping People Help You

Michelle was the chief operating officer of a company that provided very specialized, high-end executive compensation insurance products. She was charged with developing a new and highly customizable product to help stabilize executive compensation against economic uncertainty for the Central European market. That meant she needed to get up to speed on executive compensation practices in former Soviet bloc countries that were emerging as strong capitalist economies. She also needed to understand the laws governing executive compensation in those countries, and she needed to get in front of top executives of insurance companies with whom she might be able to partner in pilot projects to introduce the new product into the Central European market.

Although she was expressing her macro objective in a straightforward manner with the statement, "I need information about Central European executive compensation practices," this approach had not produced any meaningful results. Central Europe presented very interesting challenges to developing this highly customized product.

As we began to articulate her objective, we first addressed her need to gather information about executive compensation practices. We started by wondering just how many people there might be who know about executive compensation, and we got our answer—more than five hundred thousand—with an Internet search using the terms "executive compensation experts." Our review of the search results indicated that among these experts were tax specialists, human resource firms, executive compensation consultants, and attorneys specializing in compensation law, among several others. Even when we overlaid the search term "Central Europe," the number of people who might provide the information Michelle was seeking still included over ninety thousand hits. Her statement was clearly too much a macro objective; we needed to add additional micro terms that would lead her to the manageable number of results she was looking for.

As we worked on further articulating her objective, we asked ourselves what profession would know about executive compensation insurance policies. We decided to add the term "insurance broker," because insurance brokers in Central Europe would very likely have dealt with executive compensation insurance policies. Our question became "How many insurance brokers in Central Europe specialize in executive compensation packages?" This further narrowed down Michelle's search results, but she was still receiving too many hits to sift through.

Finally we decided to try to determine the top ten insurance brokers who sell executive compensation packages in Central Europe, and that search produced a very manageable number of hits. Michelle had tested her newly articulated objective to the point where she would be able to use the information she had to move forward to the next phase of the Right Person–Right Approach process.

Where Does Articulating Your Objective Lead You?

While articulating their objectives and producing a target list produced measurable results for George, Tim, Dylan, and Michelle, their results were quite different in important ways. Dylan's search led him directly to an ideal target for his macro objective: the custom automobile manufacturing company that allowed its clients to design and order their own cars over the Internet. Tim's search led him to several targets he was seeking: potential clients for his consulting services. In this case, his results had come in the form of several lists of companies with different profiles, each of which indicated it would be a likely customer. Michelle's search also led her to generate a list of people who had the information and contacts she would need in order to design and market a new executive compensation insurance package for Central European companies.

George's articulation of his objective had led him to generate only one specific target: a company that knew all about the types of decision makers he wanted to approach and that could put him in touch with them immediately. By giving him access to the person who knew precisely the business partners he needed to grow his business, George's target turned out to be the master key to fulfilling his objectives.

For most people, as was the case for Dylan, Tim, and Michelle, refining the macro objective and narrowing the list of targets doesn't take them straight to the master key. It only gets them to the next step in the process of fulfilling their objectives. They still need to gain *access* to their targets.

Chapter Four presents techniques for identifying your master key—the person (or the information that you need to connect with the person) that will give you access to the targets you've generated as a result of articulating your macro objectives clearly. I call this the "critical enabler," and it represents the "right person" part of the Right Person–Right Approach method.

CHAPTER 4

The Right Person

IDENTIFYING YOUR CRITICAL ENABLER

- *Sari was a research chemist in need of a new job, and*
- *the broadcast-your-résumé approach had not worked for*
- *her—unsurprisingly, as she was an introvert with somewhat*
- *limited English skills, and the kind of jobs where she would*
- *shine were buried in tiny labs within larger organizations.*
- *Such labs are hard for an outsider to locate. People with*
- *a general knowledge of the industry, although they may*
- *know many of their peers, don't necessarily know all of the*
- *companies that need to hire new employees—and they might*
- *be reluctant to share that information if they did. After*
- *some thought, we defined Sari's key question for finding a*
- *prospective critical enabler as "Who makes it their business*
- *to know the heads of the laboratories I'd like to work in and*
- *what their business and personnel needs might be?"*
- *After we had developed a preliminary description of the*
- *kind of laboratories Sari wanted to contact—as opposed to*
- *the specific type of job she was looking for—we asked our-*
- *selves, "OK, what do all of these laboratories have in com-*
- *mon? What do they all use? What technologies—for instance,*
- *what software, what hardware—would all of them require?"*

- *"Microscopes," Sari said at once. All of the labs would*
- *have to use the kind of microscopes known as electron spec-*
- *trometers, and they would frequently upgrade this technology.*
- *With this as a starting point, the next question was, "OK,*
- *what company manufactures these microscopes and sells them*
- *to the labs?" She had the answer to that at her fingertips too,*
- *and that led to the observation that the person most likely to*
- *deal with all of the labs Sari wanted to contact would be the*
- *sales rep who sells the microscopes to them.*
- *At that point, Sari's eyes lit up. "Oh yeah, I know him,"*
- *she said. "I bought a million dollars worth of microscopes*
- *from him three years ago."*

After refining your macro objective, narrowing down your search by identifying micro objectives, and developing a manageable list of targets—potential organizations, decision makers, or sources of information you'd like to approach—the next step is to find someone who will help you get those targets to pay attention to you. Unless you can do that, the analysis you've done so far is virtually meaningless.

The problem is that no matter what your objective, going directly to the people who can say yes or no to your request rarely works. That's because simply approaching decision makers cold, without taking the time to learn about them and differentiate yourself from others who are doing the same thing, makes you just another face in the crowd. And the more valuable and high-profile the people you want to reach, the bigger the crowd—the more requests from investors or job seekers or people needing to gather information—they're already seeing and the higher the bar to accessing them. Relying on your business plan, grant application, or résumé to communicate why your inquiry or request should be considered leaves it entirely up to the reader to see the fit, and you can't expect this level of reader to make the effort without being predisposed to work with you.

To have real influence and impact—and get results—takes more than a simple assertion that you deserve an audience. You need to surprise your decision makers by showing how well you understand their needs, interests, and objectives, and how well you can help them solve their problems. So having a referral is not enough—although you need one to get in the door, you are on your own after that. So it does you little good if you simply ride in on your referring party's coattails without knowing what to say next to engage that specific decision maker. Hence the need to find a critical enabler to arm you with the knowledge and intelligence that will allow you to captivate your decision maker. In most cases, you will need a similar round of research to select prospective critical enablers and learn enough about their needs, interests, and objectives to allow you to make an offer engaging enough to prompt at least one of them to advise you.

This sort of research can be startlingly difficult to begin. If you find yourself resisting the idea of enlisting a critical enabler, it's worth doing a reality check. Do the following thoughts seem familiar?

1. I can just tough it out and deal with this challenge on my own.

2. Asking for help is a sign of weakness.

3. Asking for help is an admission that I don't have the answer.

4. How hard could it be for me to just make the case for my great idea (or potential contribution, or whatever) on its own merits?

5. Why should I spend all this time trying to obtain background information from someone who can't make the decision?

6. How am I going to find someone who could help, and why would someone like that want to help me?

These are the mental blocks I see most often among my clients when they first contemplate the notion of a critical enabler. If you share them, consider the following insights in response:

1. You probably can, but you'll be doing it the hard way and it may take you years instead of weeks.

2. No it isn't. It is a sign of self-confidence.

3. Nothing wrong with that. The intelligence of your questions can be as impressive as having the answer.

4. Harder than you can imagine, if no one is listening, no matter how easy it feels.

5. You can't afford not to get background information if you want to succeed with the decision maker.

6. You will never know until you try. Read on . . .

How Do You Select and Engage a Critical Enabler?

What you are looking for is someone—ideally, the one best person—to provide the referral and information you need not just to get in front of each of your ultimate decision makers but to gain their serious consideration and assistance. So the goal at this stage of the Right Person–Right Approach method is to identify someone who knows everything you need to know about your target to differentiate yourself from others who might be seeking the same goal. In fact, this is so important to your success that the critical enabler is that *right person* indicated in the title of the method.

The most important attribute of a critical enabler is knowledge—the direct understanding of your targets and their field that will enable you to get to your targets quickly, easily, and efficiently. Even if you already know the decision maker you want to reach and have a referral you could invoke to arrange a meeting, chances are you would still be better off with a critical enabler who can provide the additional information, insights, or intelligence you need to make your approach effective.

How to find such a person? It's a three-step process:

1. Research your targets to determine what kinds of information about their needs, interests, and challenges you can use to shape your value proposition.

2. Research the field to identify organizations and sources most likely to generate the kinds of information

identified in Step 1; this is your pool of potential critical enablers.

3. Research the people in your pool of potential critical enablers to find the one who is most likely to make a point of knowing just what you need to know about your target and to be willing to share that intelligence with you if engaged with the right approach.

Step 1: Decide What You Need to Know About Your Target

This step involves learning what kinds of things you need to know before you can develop an approach that will surprise your targets with your perception of their needs, interests, and objectives and with your ability to tie what you need or have to offer directly to what they want. At this stage, you're not actually looking for specific information about a target; rather, you're scoping out the areas of knowledge you'll need—whether your targets are companies or people—to impress them with your approach and demonstrate that your proposal will advance their interests. And the basic question to start with boils down to, "What would enable me to prove that my value proposition is worth their consideration?"

For example, if your target is a company you'd like to work for, what do you need to learn about that company that will give you an edge when seeking employment there? Perhaps you need to learn more about the company's recent acquisitions or latest strategic initiatives. Perhaps you need to know the type of skills currently in short supply there. Regardless, this is information unlikely to be readily available from the public Web site or via an Internet search. Publicly available information is apt to be static, and the intelligence I'm referring to here is dynamic.

A command of dynamic intelligence demonstrates a true understanding of the organization or individual target, which is apt to be more impressive than anything else you could offer. It enables you to know exactly which arrow from your quiver of value propositions to use and where to aim it. That level of targeting is apt to win the following reactions:

- You must be interested enough in us to have taken the time to obtain such knowledge.

- You are well connected enough to have access to this information.

- You are concerned about the same real, higher-level issues that we are and not just interested in what you might get from us.

- I want to talk with you to find out just how on earth you found this information.

The stories in this chapter demonstrate the importance of this step and illustrate some of the ways you can go about implementing it. This step opens the way to rapidly securing resources that at first might seem unobtainable—as illustrated in the following real-life example.

Real-Life Challenge: Justify the Job

Gabe, a senior executive with a global Internet service provider, wanted to persuade a company he was interested in that it needed a chief technology officer and it should hire him for the job. The company was a venture-funded assisted living technology start-up, and the CEO wanted to create the position for him. Unfortunately, he needed approval from the investment group and the parent company's board of directors, neither of which liked the idea of adding another executive at this stage in the company's growth.

Gabe was convinced that the start-up did need a CTO, as he'd learned that it was operating without regard to two serious risks. It had only one engineer who really understood its developing product, and documentation was slim to nonexistent. It had outsourced the coding to another start-up that was also very small and in the early stages of its development—a brittle link in the supply chain that, if it failed, could bring down the whole operation. Gabe also believed that he was the right person for the job, but he needed to step back and gather additional information to quantify the exposure associated with both these risks before making his case to the company's board and to its investors.

Quantifying the risk would allow him to demonstrate to his potential employer that his services were needed to develop policies and practices that would enable the company to reduce its exposure significantly, thus buttressing his credentials and reinforcing the reasons the company should hire him. The process would also allow him to double-check his initial decision to take the position if it was offered to him, given the risks he was becoming aware of. He needed to do significant research to address both of these issues.

Gabe realized that he needed to find examples of companies that had gone out of business because they hadn't developed a way to anticipate potential emergencies like the ones he had uncovered. That insight was the key to the first step in identifying a critical enabler: he'd discovered what he didn't know.

What you don't know certainly can hurt you, and identifying it is an important step in finding the critical enabler—the person who has the knowledge you need.

Step 2: Locate the Intelligence You Need

Once you've found out what you need to know about your target or targets—the kinds of intelligence that will give you the sort of "unfair advantage" so much admired and desired in business—the next step is identifying the kinds of people who have this knowledge. To generate a short list of places to find people who may have the intelligence you need, ask yourself these questions:

- "Where can I find people who have already accomplished the objective I'm looking to achieve?"

Someone out there has already done this before; you just have to find them. Look at the organizations in your network to see if they contain anyone with experience you'd like to emulate.

- "Where can I find people who study, write about, track, or otherwise follow what it is that I'm trying to do?"

Someone out there probably has already studied the people who have done what you're trying to do, so you need to find out where the experts hang out. For example, www.xcomomy.com has a cadre of thought leaders it calls "Xconomists" who specialize in studying the so-called exponential economies—genomics, genetics, Web semantics, nanotechnology, and any other industry that starts growing at an exponential rate. Look at investors, search professionals, trade journal editors, consultants, places where thought leaders publish their work. These fields will very frequently include people able to provide the information you seek, or to direct you to others who can.

- "Where can I find people who review value propositions like mine?"

Someone out there has worked on projects resembling yours. Consider the types of advisers likely to become involved as you approach your objective. People who have been drawn into this type of activity on other projects may well have the knowledge you want in your critical enabler, so it's useful to develop a list of professions and specialties that work with the kind of objective you're trying to achieve. For example, if you're seeking a grant, you can look at organizations who have already landed grants, attorneys who provide legal counsel to people developing grants, and consultants who help with grant development.

Applying for a job, obtaining regulatory approval, penetrating a new market, hiring a new employee, doing due diligence in preparation for an acquisition, starting a new company—no matter what you're trying to accomplish, there's someone out there who has the intelligence you need to accomplish your goal. When you've finished Step 2, you'll have generated a list of potential sources of critical enablers. My client Alyssa's experience is a great example of the power of this step.

Real-Life Challenge: An Embarrassment of Riches

"I don't know where to start when I present this product," Alyssa told me. She had identified dozens of potential targets in the financial services industry—possible customers for her company's customer relationship management software. Her task was to determine how best to approach these targets, but companies could realize such a wide variety of benefits by installing her company's software that she felt she had no way to predict which benefits would appeal to any given stakeholder. This challenge was compounded by the sheer number of stakeholders; the target companies she'd identified often had dozens of decision makers with a voice in the selection, and she was having difficulty finding ways to tailor her presentations to the unique needs of each of the decision makers. She could go to each potential customer and try the shotgun approach, displaying all the benefits at once, but she realized that she'd already encountered too many blank stares when she made this type of all-or-nothing pitch.

The first question I asked her was, "Is there an overall problem that your product addresses?" She thought about this, then said, "It addresses the problem of how to stop losing customers." My next question focused on helping her discover key information about her targets that would enable her to tailor her sales presentation to this specific problem: I asked her what she'd love to know about her target companies—that is, what would help her identify the ones that truly had a need for her product. She answered, "What I'd love to know about these guys is, which ones have recently experienced significant losses of customers? Where have they lost customers? Which ones have lost customers because their communications and customer service were so poor? If I can find this out, I can really tailor my presentation to a specific set of problems."

Once she'd identified the knowledge she needed to acquire, I asked, "Who would know what companies in the financial services industry are losing business? And further, who would know why they're losing business?" In other words, who makes it their business to address different aspects of the same basic problem her company addresses? Alyssa immediately identified a consulting firm that companies such as the ones she wanted to sell to hired in precisely the type of situation she had specified. It specialized in exit interviews with customers who had terminated their relationships, reporting back to its clients the reasons their clients were leaving. By identifying the organization that would have the information she was seeking, Alyssa had generated her list of potential critical enablers. She was ready to move on to the third step in this process, screening her critical enabler pool to identify a specific person in the organization she could approach to obtain the information she needed.

Once you know what you want to know, you need to figure out where to look for it. It doesn't work to simply talk to anyone about the information you are seeking. If you just start reaching out to people at random, you're more likely to be fishing in a bathtub than in a well-stocked pond.

Step 3: Screen the Pool of Potential Critical Enablers

The final step in identifying the right critical enabler is to look through your pool and assess how likely each of your prospects is to have the information you're looking for. First, query your network to see if someone knows the person you're considering. I find that frequently people are surprised to find they know someone who is in some way associated with the prospect or can recommend someone else who is so they can generate a referral (and some background information) that way. The old "six degrees of separation" idea may not feel true when you're in the midst of pursuing a difficult objective, but it reflects a very real level of interconnection in the modern world.

In addition, you can look at the American Society of Association Executives (www.asaecenter.org) and the Gale directory for your field (www.gale.cengage.com/Directory Library/) to find out which professional organizations your prospect belongs to. If you see that your prospect will be attending a meeting or a conference of the organization, you can try to arrange a casual meeting there to get a sense of the knowledge that might be available from that source. You might also call the Membership Chair at the professional organization to see if they would recommend the prospect as having the knowledge you're seeking.

You can also search the Internet to find information about the level of knowledge or expertise your potential critical enabler possesses. Search on keywords related to your field of interest and your prospect's name. Has your prospect been quoted or published papers or other work, including Internet blogs, that indicate the level of expertise you're seeking? Has your prospect posted about the type of project or situation you have in mind? In other words, is your potential critical enabler experienced or considered to be a thought leader in the area you're exploring?

Remember that your focus here is on discovering whether the potential critical enabler has the knowledge you're seeking. This indirect screening process is designed to reduce the pool of prospects to the few who meet your criteria exactly, or to the smallest number of people who collectively cover the criteria. The ideal is to identify the single right person to help you reach your objective, as Sari did, but it's also possible to work with two or more people if no one critical enabler who will talk to you has everything you need. In some cases, one source will be best for background information, whereas another has the position to provide a referral. Consider a couple of real-life examples.

Real-Life Challenge: Aim for the Bull's-Eye
Tyler had secured the right to license a newly developed microchip that dramatically improved the recharge rate

of optical devices, allowing them to capture new images without delay. He had developed a business plan and identified several targets—venture capital firms he wanted to approach—and he was naturally eager to submit his business plan to all of them. But he had more work to do before he could approach investors with his best foot forward.

"What are these investors really looking for?" I asked him.

"Ways to make money," he said.

That was too general, I explained. Instead, he needed to find his targets' underlying investment criteria and tailor his proposal to each of them. Without doing the research to satisfy this need and differentiate the proposal significantly from those of others approaching the same target, he'd be saying, in effect, "Here's my business plan; I hope you like it. I hope you can figure out on your own how it fits your investment strategy and complements your existing portfolio of companies."

We continued our research by studying his targets' portfolio companies, looking for any kind of connection between them and Tyler's microchip. Within a few hours, an answer jumped out at us. One of his targets had invested in a company that manufactured night vision goggles and binoculars. "Wow," Tyler said, "this is a perfect fit! My technology could improve this product immeasurably, and I'm sure he'd be happy to help me get the business off the ground so I could supply it to him."

But we didn't stop there. Deepening our exploration of this target's portfolio, Tyler recognized the name of an old acquaintance on the management team of another of the portfolio companies. "Sam will talk with me," he said.

"Why?" I asked. I pointed out that just being friends with people doesn't guarantee that they'll go out of their way to help you.

"We worked at the same company a few years ago, and he knows he can call on me if he needs help," he replied.

This gave him a chain of potential critical enablers. His goal with his former coworker Sam would be to gain an introduction to the CEO of the night optics company. The technological fit would provide an incentive for the night optics CEO to serve as a critical enabler with the investor.

The intelligence and referrals developed from this chain of critical enablers put Tyler in a position to develop a value proposition tailored exactly to this target investor's needs. The difference it made was immense. As Tyler put it, "I never realized how important identifying the bull's-eye within my target was!"

Real-Life Challenge: Find Out How Things Really Work

Nicholas was building his own consulting firm, after working as a Wall Street analyst and director of research in a top firm that specialized in the software industry. He knew that a major software firm was looking for ways to compete in the race to acquire smaller companies in order to increase its product line and market share within the industry. The company's main competitor had an extremely effective acquisition process, and the company Nicholas wanted as a client needed to get its acquisitions process up to speed if it hoped to compete. In particular, Nicholas believed his target company needed to develop a methodology for analyzing and determining in advance the likelihood that the culture of the company to be acquired would be easily grafted onto the culture of the acquiring company.

We determined that Nicholas needed to know about the mergers and acquisitions process that his target company had been following in order to articulate the company's problems and to pair his relevant experience accordingly. Once we'd determined what he didn't know, the next step was to identify a pool of people who might have that information. We refined his description of his needs by asking what companies Nicholas knew of that had been courted—or acquired—by his target company. He also knew that he could obtain valuable information from anyone who had been associated in any way with his target's mergers and acquisitions process, including attorneys, accountants, and business brokers. In short, he wanted to gather insight into the process that his target company invoked when attempting to acquire another organization—but he did not want to interview *everyone* who met those criteria.

As usual, asking the right question led to the right answer. Until Nicholas asked the question that unlocked the information he needed, he'd been at a dead end. Now he began flipping through his network, where he discovered nearly a dozen people who had either worked for his target company or been exposed to its mergers and acquisitions process. They were people he'd always known, but he now saw them in a new light based on the information needs he'd identified.

In this case, Nicholas determined that no one of his potential critical enablers had all of the intelligence he needed to acquire. Rather, each of them possessed some of it. Instead of screening his list to find exactly the right person, he decided to talk systematically with several prospects from his list to capture various angles of intelligence that he would then assemble into his overview of the mergers and acquisitions process at his target company.

As with the other techniques in the Right Person–Right Approach method, searching for a critical enabler is not a magic wand. But as long as you are pursuing an objective that is within your ability, someone out there can help you clear the way to it. It's only necessary to take the time to find them.

So What Defines *Your* Critical Enabler?

Once you begin thinking in terms of finding a critical enabler instead of approaching a decision maker directly, your whole outlook changes. The world really is full of people who could help you get where you want to go—and will do so if you discover what you can offer to make the exchange mutually beneficial. But to get what you want, you have to know what you want. And once you've identified what you want in a critical enabler, you may be surprised how many can be found in your own backyard—and even in your own network.

Whether or not you already know your critical enabler, however, it's important to approach that person in the right way. One of the biggest mistakes you can make is to glibly assume, "Oh, we're buddies. He'll share what he knows with me." Never take a relationship for granted. I've seen people withhold information from their best friends because they're worried, for instance, that having the information get out might not reflect well on them, or because they're worried about how their friend might use the information.

Instead, treat every potential critical enabler as someone who needs to be strategically approached and properly motivated to share information, regardless of your prior relationship. Chapter Six goes into more detail on how to approach a prospective critical enabler the right way. If you already have a critical enabler in mind and either a dramatic offer or some prior goodwill established, as Tyler did with his two prospects, developing the "reason" for them to help you is the next step.

But what happens if you've identified your ideal critical enabler and your connection is remote or nonexistent? Then you'll need a referral to that person—the topic of Chapter Five.

CHAPTER 5

The Referral

LANDING AN INTRODUCTION TO
A CRITICAL ENABLER

- Cyril was looking to buy small manufacturing companies,
- and he'd identified one he wanted to acquire. He'd also iden-
- tified as his prospective critical enabler a man named Josiah,
- the president of a tool-and-die manufacturing firm that
- supplied equipment to his target company, who was sure to
- have valuable background information that would help him
- approach the CEO of the company he was interested in.
-     Cyril was connected to Josiah through Diane, whom
- he'd met casually. He wanted to get a referral to his prospect
- from Diane, but because he didn't know Diane well, he was
- hesitant to ask. This is the classic LinkedIn conundrum.
- How do you get a referral from someone you know to some-
- one they know? Suddenly two degrees away feels like six
- degrees away.
-     His approach to Diane went something like this: after
- mentioning a conference they'd both attended a while back,
- Cyril said he was evaluating a number of small manufactur-
- ing firms with a view to acquisition, and one of the people
- he'd really like to ask for advice about them was Josiah, who
- showed up as a connection of Diane's on LinkedIn.

- "I don't feel I know you well enough to ask you for a
- formal referral," Cyril said, "but I was wondering if you'd
- be willing to let me mention your name when I contact
- Josiah. It will make it easier to meet him if I can start by
- establishing that we simply have a mutual acquaintance."
- After gathering a bit more information about why Cyril
- wanted to see Josiah, Diane said, "Sure, I'm comfortable
- with that. Do you want me to contact him for you?"
- Cyril explained that he'd be happy if Diane gave Josiah
- a heads-up, but he wanted to gather more information about
- Josiah and his company in order to develop a well-thought-
- out approach. He promised to drop Diane a note a few days
- before he'd be ready to write to Josiah.

Once you've screened your pool of potential critical enablers and identified the one you want to approach, the question becomes the age-old *How do I get in to see this person?* The answer is just as old: you get a referral from someone who knows your prospect.

For some people, referrals are such a staple of business life that they're easy to take for granted. Unfortunately, the traditional referral process is fraught with subtle problems that make it far less effective and harder than it could be. And it is very difficult to measure the success or failure of a referral—as long as you get one and get in to see your target, it's easy to proceed without realizing that even though the process appeared to be seamless and successful, you may have paid a high price. The full potential value, impact, and effect of a referral is squandered if you think of it as only a way to get in. The real value is realized when a referral is combined with control and intelligence. Although you may say "Yippee!" when someone tells you about a hot fishing hole, you still can easily waste that opportunity if you forget to ask (or find out on your own or from another source) what the fish are biting on and when.

For others, just the thought of getting a referral seems intimidating. As one of my clients told me, "I know so few people; who am I going to ask? I wish the referral process were a problem I could worry about!" But with the process outlined in this chapter, you can generate referrals you didn't know you had access to, fairly easily. And these will not be the traditional referrals, and they will not carry the traditional price.

The price of a traditional referral tends to come in the form of issues that remain below the surface. Here are a few of the reasons the referrals you've received or generated might not have been as effective as you thought, even when they did lead to a meeting:

- *Nonendorsement:* The recipient assumed the person who provided the referral was also providing an endorsement or recommendation at the same time. Unfortunately, it often turns out that referring parties don't actually vouch for the people they refer—they understandably use cautious terms to cover themselves in case the meeting doesn't go well. As a result, even a target who agrees to a meeting does so with reservations.

- *Misdirected Messenger:* The recipient allowed the person giving the referral to approach the target, passing along the résumé or business plan or whatever documentation was designed to support the hoped-for request. But the referring party doesn't make a vivid case. The documentation winds up being forwarded to human resources or tossed onto a pile to be reviewed later, and the target doesn't take the initiative to invite the recipient to meet.

- *Coattail Comfort:* The recipient thought the referring party's name would open the door and provide an "in," with no need to demonstrate further initiative or resourcefulness. But "Joe sent me" hasn't worked since the last speakeasy closed; it's far more effective to make it clear why the referral is worthwhile, and those who expect their target to welcome them with open arms, purely on the basis of the referral, are often disappointed.

Thus even when it may appear that the referral has generated the results the recipient was looking for, it may in fact have fallen short. Your long-term results are apt to be far better if you keep the process in your own hands, as Cyril did. Remember that the referral alone is only part of the entrance fee. It's not enough to say, "I'm writing to you because Joe said I should"; the message is much likelier to get through if you say, "I'm very interested in what you are doing—and Joe, whom we both know, agreed that I should reach out to you."

Rather than asking or simply allowing referring parties to present you to your target or pass along documents for the target to see, it's better to say you would prefer not to impose on them in that fashion or that you don't expect them to do your work for you. They don't need to endorse you or get you an interview—just allow you to mention them as part of demonstrating a more comprehensive, thoughtful, and educated approach.

How Do You Manage Referrals?

Rather than leaving referrals essentially under the control of someone else, the Right Person–Right Approach method puts you in control of referrals, or at least in the position of managing them very carefully. This allows you to avoid the many hidden pitfalls in the traditional referral process. These are the three features that make the difference:

- You make it easy for your referring party to give you a referral by making it clear you are not asking for an endorsement or recommendation.

- You use the discussion of a possible referral to gather additional information about your prospective critical enabler.

- You contact the person you're referred to yourself, rather than waiting for the referring party to somehow generate an invitation for you.

Making It Easy

Your initial task with people you're asking for referrals is to realign their expectations so they understand what you're really asking of them—which is *not* to present your credentials or to appear to be your sponsor or (worse yet) your agent.

All you're asking from referrers is permission to use their names. Once people understand that you're not asking them to do your work for you, or really to do very much at all, you'll generally find they become much more willing to help you. But because most people will assume that you are asking for a recommendation when you're looking for a referral, you do need to preface the conversation in a way that makes it clear you're not asking for the moon.

At the same time, you also need to assure people that you understand that the referral needs to reflect well on their judgment. Make it clear that you mean to do your homework, so that your communication with your target demonstrates your informed and intelligent interest and potential usefulness.

Assure your referrers that you will send them copies of any correspondence that mentions them by name. That way, they'll know that you've stuck to your word.

Let's take a look at how one of my clients successfully managed a referral.

Real-Life Challenge: Create an Introduction

John, a sales rep, knew that the components his employer produced had improved to the point where they would stand up to large-scale use by a major manufacturer of consumer electronics. However, his target's online procurement processes were extremely convoluted, and he thought he could make progress much more quickly if he could just talk with Carolyn, the procurement director.

He had no connection to anyone at the target company, but an old friend of his named Fred was connected through Facebook to a woman named Laura, who held a position high up in customer service there. With any luck, she'd know how to reach Carolyn—but how to get to Laura?

John met with Fred and, after chewing over old times a bit, said, "I noticed you've got a Facebook connection to Laura, who's in customer service at XYZ Company." He explained that he wanted to talk with her in hopes of getting an introduction to Carolyn, in procurement at XYZ, because he was sure the company would be interested in his components if he could only present them in person.

"Sorry, John," Fred replied. "I don't really know her all that well, and I don't feel I'm in a position to recommend anyone to her. Why don't you just go to their Web site and run through the application section there?"

"I've done all that—it's like standing in line for a movie that may not open after all. What I really want is to talk with someone at XYZ who can tell me a little about what they really need, so I'm not just making a generic case."

Fred reiterated that he really didn't know Laura well enough to make an introduction—and he didn't know John's products all that well either, if it came to a recommendation.

"But you don't need to do any of that," John replied. "It's my job to put the meeting together if I can. All I really need is to be able to mention the name of a mutual acquaintance when I reach out to her. May I just say I was talking with you, and you agreed that it wouldn't hurt if I tried contacting her directly?"

"Well, in that context, I don't mind at all if you use my name," said Fred.

John's message to Laura went like this:

> Subject: Our mutual acquaintance, Fred . . .
>
> Dear Laura,
>
> I was just talking with our mutual acquaintance Fred So-and-so, who agreed it would be a good idea for me to approach Carolyn in XYZ Procurement directly. I've already filled out the automated RFP form, but I'd love to differentiate my company with a more personalized approach—and I'm afraid she's so busy my note would just get lost in the shuffle. If you know Carolyn, I'd be grateful if you'd be willing to share some insight into what she needs.

Laura was intrigued enough to talk with John, and eventually permitted him to name her as an acquaintance when he wrote to Carolyn.

Spreading Your Nets

One reason the Right Person–Right Approach method has you work with a critical enabler is to gather important intelligence about the decision makers you're ultimately approaching and the issues important to them, so that you can differentiate yourself from others blindly seeking similar goals. In a sense, when you work with a referrer to get through to a prospective critical enabler, you need to do a scaled-down version of the same thing—gather as much information as you can about the person you hope to engage as your critical enabler. The people who can provide useful referrals are in many cases the ones most likely to have the information you need. Yet all too often, the singular goal of obtaining the referral limits the potential additional value the referring party can provide. Unless you ask, that referring party is unlikely to think of volunteering additional information.

Although many people I introduce this strategy to respond with the concern that it's asking too much of the referring party, I've found that a discussion designed to elicit this information will actually impress the referrer with the thoughtfulness and care with which you intend to handle the referral. Meanwhile, assembling the information will help your referrer understand that you will make them look very good when you contact your prospective critical enabler. This addresses the typical subconscious concern a referrer harbors, worrying whether the one contacted as a result of the referral will perceive it as a favor received or requested.

But you're unlikely to get this kind of information unless you ask for it. In the traditional referral process, all the value and weight is attached to the referral itself, and people asked for referrals tend to stick to yes or no, without considering anything else that might be useful. So ask about what your prospective critical enablers need, value, or appreciate—strategic goals they're pursuing, projects they have in the works, problems they've encountered and are trying to solve. Somewhere within the answers to such questions you are likely to find a clue, something that you can speak to in your proposition that surprises the recipient with what you have obviously taken the time to learn.

The following story illustrates a way to begin gathering the initial information you need as you begin to build your approach to your critical enabler.

Real-Life Challenge: Find Potential Customers

Clayton had written a book promoting a new method he'd developed for capitalizing nonprofit corporations. His business objective was to be able to present his method in person to the heads of nonprofits, and he'd identified Barry, the manager of a large charitable investment fund that works with such organizations, as his critical enabler. He didn't know Barry, but he had found someone to provide a referral.

"I appreciate your giving me the referral to Barry," Clayton told that someone, "but I'd actually like to tailor my approach a bit, rather than just take the lazy way out and send everything I have, leaving it up to him to pore through my materials to find the fit. Could you take a few minutes to talk with me about him—his interests, what his challenges are, what kinds of things motivate him? I'm hoping to be able to approach him with a more specific, up-front offer of help or information that would make his life easier, or somehow help him do his job better."

The referring party found this inquiry refreshing and considerate, and he welcomed the opportunity to share his background knowledge. He provided enough information about how Barry got most of his business leads for the lightbulb to go off in Clayton's head about a key introduction that was quite likely to be welcome. As Clayton thanked the referrer, he mentioned that it would be several days before he'd be contacting Barry, but that he'd let the referrer know when he did so.

Taking the Initiative

Although a brief heads-up call at the right time can help pave the way for you, the referrer's name is all that really matters. Name recognition is the most important aspect of the referral in the Right Person–Right Approach method. It's what gets the attention of the prospective critical enabler, and it opens the door for you to make your presentation without relinquishing control of the process to someone else. It takes remarkably little to differentiate yourself from the masses when it comes to referrals.

Although most people you ask for casual referrals will think the best way to help you is to contact the party they're referring you to and give them a heads-up that you're going to call, this isn't necessarily useful if the call arrives two weeks before you're ready to begin talking with your prospective critical enabler. Once you get a referral, you'll generally still have additional research to do on your prospect to find out how best to demonstrate that your proposition fits their needs. Try to make sure that if your referring party insists on calling your prospect in advance, the call doesn't come before you're ready. It is easy to feel obligated to act immediately on a gracious referral. However, the referring party will respect you even more when you explain your desire to make the most of that referral—which includes doing everything you can to learn about the person they refer you to.

When you're using the Right Person–Right Approach method, you contact your prospective critical enabler yourself. You can use only the name of the referring party without implying that there's any recommendation in the exchange. Remember that the behavior you display in your communications says as much about who you are as anything you can say in a résumé or proposal, if not more—for one thing, it's what the people you talk to will notice. In your approach to your prospect, highlight two or three things that will demonstrate knowledge of the prospect's aims—and your willingness and attempt to help advance those aims.

I've found that most people appreciate an e-mail message first, explaining who the referring party was and the reason for the inquiry. To retain control, wind up the message with a statement like "I'll follow up shortly by phone to see if it makes sense to meet." When you do phone, chances are the recipient will recognize you from having read the message prior to the call. If not, you can cite the date and ask if they want to review it to get the gist of your inquiry first. Here's an example of how this works.

Real-Life Challenge: Stand Out from the Crowd

Tony was eager to get into hedge fund management as soon as he completed his master's in finance, and he was sure that one of his professors would be an ideal critical enabler for him. He'd researched a fund the professor had written about, and he thought he saw a major area where his own research could be useful. Unfortunately, the professor—a superstar who'd held high government office and was still active in various types of consulting—was in such demand that his classes were crowded and it was very difficult to catch his eye, let alone talk to him seriously. He was notoriously reluctant to provide referrals or recommendations for students; when people offered to give him résumés, he would either shunt them aside or offer to send them on without showing much interest.

Rather than join the group hovering around after class, Tony went to his faculty adviser and asked if she would help pave the way for him. "Sure," she said. "I'll give him a call and see if I can send him your résumé."

"That'd be great," Tony replied, "but it isn't really necessary. If I can just send him a message with a subject line like 'Dr. Andrews suggested'—or even just 'agreed'—'that I talk to you,' I think that would get his attention. I've been working on a spreadsheet analyzing market behavior in Latin America, and I think he'd be interested."

She agreed that it would be OK for him to do that, and she asked him to keep her posted.

Tony then wrote to the professor and described his interest in hedge funds and their need for more quantitative analysis. He offered to share his spreadsheet—describing some of its predictive power—and asked if it would be possible to get together for a few minutes some afternoon. The professor agreed to sit down over coffee, and after talking for a while, he asked whether Tony was looking for an introduction to someone at the hedge fund they'd been discussing.

"I appreciate the thought," Tony said. "But I don't expect you to do my job for me. I figure it's my job to get an interview, but I really appreciate what you're telling me about this fund—it'll allow me to send a cover letter that reflects some real understanding of their strategy and needs and points out my relevant experience." He asked if it would be OK to say in the letter that he was one of the professor's students and that they'd discussed hedge funds—not claiming a referral, just using the name. He promised to send the professor a copy of the letter, and the professor authorized him to send it.

By maintaining control over the process, Tony was able to present himself to the hedge fund (which eventually hired him) at a time of his own choosing. He improved his reception there by revealing his interest, initiative, resourcefulness, communications skills, and problem-solving ability through his own actions—his approach demonstrated these qualities, so he didn't need to write anything claiming them.

What Does It Look Like from the Other Side?

Sometimes it seems like my whole business life consists of making referrals. That's what has led me to spend so much time analyzing the referral process.

Early in my career, being an undisciplined connector, I was somewhat reckless about making and accepting requests for referrals. I would happily take over and shepherd the referral from one person to another. Being the one in control, I inserted myself into the process as the go-between. But often I later regretted volunteering to be the facilitator, because that meant I had to follow up and to deliver on the implied promise of a meeting. And at the end of the day, I simply didn't have the same motivation to follow through and make things happen as the person who requested the referral would have had.

Then I learned a key lesson: losing control is a good thing. I eventually realized that by taking control of the process I actually disempowered the people being referred. I deprived them of the chance to impress the people I referred them to based on their approach. They were left with no way to differentiate themselves other than by being referred by me.

The relationship was not healthy because the people seeking referrals were solely dependent on me to deliver a meeting. Had I instead allowed them to initiate the communication, armed with my additional information about the one they were to meet, it would have been a healthy *interdependent* relationship.

I've come to regard the concept of interdependence as one of the key elements of my work. My friend Cliff Hakim introduced me to it in his book *We Are All Self-Employed*, in which he describes it as part of what he regards as the new social contract for work in today's world. "Today each of us must take full responsibility for our career mobility and job productivity," he says. His call for striking an interdependent balance between precarious dependence and lone-warrior independence applies to many business and life situations—not least to the situation my clients find themselves in.

These days, my clients do their part. They identify anything else they can come up with about the people I refer them to, and they also handle the legwork of approaching these people. Meanwhile, I stick to my easier part by lending them my name and providing key additional information, increasing their ability to associate and identify with the target. Yes, in some cases I might give the target a heads-up about the referral, but otherwise I keep my hands off. The shift in control has represented another important benefit. As I migrated from being coach to being coach and agent, I had to make sure every referral was viewed by both parties as nothing other than brilliant. This allowed me to say to clients, "Here is someone I think could help you enormously. However, I can't make the referral until you have learned enough about the person and their business so you can add value to the process. Making you jump through this hoop will ensure that you carry your own weight and eliminate any risk of it backfiring for me."

And everyone wins. I do less but look better in the process, because the people I refer now show initiative by taking an educated and thoughtful approach. That allows them to be more impressive, on their own, than they would be if I acted as their messenger. And that means I am now associated with making referrals for impressive people: the ones who take the initiative and are thoughtful in the referral process.

Real-Life Challenge: Dig Ever Deeper

The traditional referral process is worth a closer look, if only to illustrate what can go wrong when things get out of hand. As happened to my client Susanne.

Susanne had gotten a referral to the head of a department at a company she really wanted to work for. Unfortunately, the referral hadn't worked—she hadn't been offered an interview, even though she'd been referred by a big wheel in the company.

I asked her to tell me more about what had happened. She explained that her uncle Matt had suggested she call Sam, a vice president at the company. This seemed really promising. Susanne thought she had it made.

When Susanne told Sam that her uncle Matt had suggested it, Sam asked, "How is old Matt? I haven't seen him for quite a while, but we go way back." He then told Susanne to send along her résumé and he'd personally forward it to the department head Susanne wanted to meet with. Susanne thanked him, sent off an e-mail with her résumé attached, and waited for a call. And waited. Two weeks elapsed, and the call still hadn't come in.

What had gone wrong? Susanne couldn't find out. Her uncle Matt told her he didn't feel right about calling his friend Sam to ask why his niece hadn't gotten in for an interview. "It would seem like I was implying that he hadn't done what he told me he would do," was how Matt put it. "Plus, it would make it look like I was saying he didn't have much clout with the higher-ups."

Susanne herself didn't know Sam at all and felt that calling him would make her look pushy—compromising their relationship, tenuous though it might be. She didn't want to damage any goodwill Sam might have held for her by questioning him in any way.

For Susanne, as for many others caught in referral limbo, uncovering the details was impossible, but the outline of the problem was clear—Susanne had lost control over the referral process, and in doing so had lost control over achieving her business objective. It was easy to count the ways in which this referral almost certainly went wrong:

- Giving the documentation to the referring party
- Leaving the referring party to make contact with the target and to present the documentation without further reference to the one being referred
- Failing to take the opportunity to get to know more about the target
- Assuming that the referral would come with a warm endorsement

What generally happens in this sort of situation is that once referring parties are in control, they feel they need to protect themselves from a potential backlash, one that can cast a shadow on their judgment and risk their own relationship capital. So in the interest of self-protection, they're apt to be reluctant to say, "Oh, I hear she's really good," because if the meeting or interview is a bust, their own credibility takes a hit. Somebody in Sam's position is more likely to say, "I don't know this woman at all, but here's her résumé. I know her uncle, and I told him I'd pass it along to you." No wonder Susanne didn't get a call back.

In this kind of scenario, both parties wind up feeling uncomfortable and regretting the whole thing. The party getting the referral squirms about the persistence it takes to chase down the one giving it. The one giving the referral regrets having overcommitted and now underdelivering and wishes the whole thing hadn't come up. It isn't that people don't want to help, or even to follow through, but they don't know the easy way to make it happen.

Once you've gotten referred to your critical enabler, you're ready to take the next step in the process of accomplishing your business objective: making the right approach. The right approach consists of making a gesture of progressive reciprocity to engage the interest and support of your prospective critical enabler. This is the subject of the next chapter.

CHAPTER 6
The Right Approach

PROVIDING VALUE TO YOUR CRITICAL ENABLER

As a commercial real estate agent, Lorrie developed a passionate interest in the technology used to boost the energy efficiency of the buildings whose sales she had brokered for many years. She wanted to get out of large commercial real estate asset management and brokerage and become an independent consultant, providing advisory services on green energy solutions for commercial real estate tenants and property owners.

To assemble the knowledge base such a consultancy would need, Lorrie knew she had to get in front of—and up to speed on—as many new technology companies as possible. Unfortunately, the industry was developing so rapidly and was so decentralized that it was tough to track down the requisite intelligence.

Lorrie had identified a prospective critical enabler, the founder of a progressive general contracting firm that helped companies retrofit their buildings with energy-saving technologies such as solar energy panels and geothermal heat pumps—exactly the kinds of companies Lorrie would be targeting as she built her consulting business. However, Lorrie

- told me she couldn't see why on earth this critical enabler
- would want to share the enormous amount of green indus-
- try intelligence he possessed. All I could say was, be patient,
- or have faith, or just trust me on this one—we'll figure out a
- way to have this guy eating out of your hand.

- In brainstorming her gesture of progressive reciprocity,
- we asked, "What is the overlap between the industries this
- prospect targets and the ones you have relationships with as
- a result of your work as a commercial real estate agent?"
- We searched the company's client list on its Web site and dis-
- covered that it was targeting many industries, from health
- care to manufacturing, but had only one academic institu-
- tion as a client. Lorrie had done a great deal of development
- work with academic institutions in the area, so it looked like
- this was an area where she could help this prospect.

- Lorrie identified one college in particular that she knew
- was in the midst of a major capital campaign for the "green-
- ovation" of several buildings on campus, which it hoped
- to get certified as energy-efficient by the leading standards
- organization in the industry. Lorrie called her contact at
- the college to talk about the renovation plans and find out
- whether a contractor had been chosen for that aspect of the
- work. Not only had the college not selected a contractor,
- Lorrie learned, but its understanding of what needed to be
- done in this area also needed a major upgrade.

- Lorrie got a referral to her prospect, and in her initial e-mail,
- along with her request for help evaluating cutting-edge energy
- efficiency technologies, she mentioned that she could likely
- help them get more business in the academic market. Lorrie
- explained that she was doing green energy consulting, advising

- *clients about the technologies that were becoming available,*
- *and that she'd identified a potential client for her prospect's*
- *company at a local university. Her prospect was very inter-*
- *ested and scheduled the meeting at once. Lorrie's ability to*
- *help her prospect expand his market led to a fruitful partner-*
- *ship in which she was able to expand the clientele for her con-*
- *sulting business in exchange for helping her critical enabler*
- *expand his clientele. It turned into, as Lorrie phrased it, a*
- *"mutual critical enabler relationship."*

Once you've identified a prospective critical enabler and generated a referral to that person, the next step is to select the most effective approach—what you can say that will truly motivate the person to want to help you. If you want people to want to help you, it's not enough to simply call or send e-mail and expect the recipients to jump at the chance, even if they are obligated to take your call based on some previous connection or relationship. And simply mentioning the name of your referring party is likely not enough at this stage, either. To make it likely that your prospective critical enabler really will be eager to help you, you need to deploy one of the most powerful weapons in your arsenal: the gesture of progressive reciprocity.

Of course, the concept of reciprocity has been fundamental to getting business done since business began getting done. Gestures of reciprocity—thanks, tips in money or information, offers of assistance—acknowledge indebtedness and offer payback. And although modern customs (and laws) frown on *demands* for such gestures and on exchanges of too concrete a value, when properly framed they remain a legitimate and powerful lubricant for keeping the wheels of society moving.

The Right Person–Right Approach method puts a new twist on the concept by turning it into progressive reciprocity. That is, rather than offering something out of a sense of obligation after you've made a request or accepted an offer, you do so in your introductory communication, *before* you ask your prospective critical enabler for what you need. And if done in a genuine, well-researched manner, this step identifies you as a giver rather than a taker, the real key to making people willing to help you rather than to just throw you a bone.

Where Do You Start?

The first thing you must do is some general research to discover the intersection between your prospective critical enabler's possible needs and what you could possibly offer. Learn enough about your prospect's business or other interests to determine what type of gesture might offer value. Social media have made this process vastly easier than ever before, yet few people take advantage of the opportunity. Reciprocity gems will be found from simple Web searches, social network site lookups, and querying your own network to find other people who know your prospect.

Once you've done initial research, examine your own interests and pursuits and contacts, looking for ways they connect with those of your prospect. This is what I call your "inventorying reciprocity currency," something that you have or can easily obtain or can make happen that will be of value to the people you're approaching. Reciprocity currency can take many forms—a contact that would be of value to them or knowledge they might need. In some cases it can be something not directly related to your critical enabler's business or practice. What people find most surprising when they start to think hard about a gesture of progressive reciprocity is that they really don't have to think all that hard. Most of us are sitting on a reserve of reciprocity currency that we never think to inventory and fully realize. So it's important to understand how much of a reserve you can actually call on in order to smooth your way to your career and business objectives. Very often it is simply based on the common ground between you and your prospective critical enabler that your research uncovers.

When I explain the concept of progressive reciprocity to clients and friends, some initially balk at the idea. It can seem unpalatable or impractical and even contrived, especially if you're trying to develop a gesture based on information about an industry or a market segment or a technology you know little or nothing about, or when you're trying to approach a very important or accomplished person you hope will become your critical enabler. *Who am I to think I could offer anything of value to this expert?* people think. *After all, he is the master, and I am just a grasshopper.* But bear in mind that what you might be able to offer doesn't have to be in your sole possession. You can consider your network as an extension of your value. Some of the most valuable gestures of progressive reciprocity can be the easiest to deliver—if you make the right introduction, both parties will feel you've done them favors. So when you're developing a gesture of progressive reciprocity, don't limit yourself to what *you* know or can offer directly.

If you can't find the right gesture initially, don't give up on progressive reciprocity. You can create your own reciprocity currency, as most of the people I've worked with have discovered. If you're talking with someone who doesn't seem interested in your first offer, you can simply ask whether there's anything you can do. Say you like to keep the scales even and you hope there's some way you can help. Your prospect will probably say, "Oh no, I'm fine." But if you prompt for more detail, something may well crop up, and even if it doesn't, the attitude of willingness will often leave your prospect disposed to help you.

As you move forward, keep in mind that this process can frequently be quite flexible and indirect. Many of my clients' gestures are developed through bringing people together in combinations that came to mind only after they'd freed themselves of preconceptions about what might be valuable to their critical enablers.

Finally, remember that you're not hiring on as a consultant. Your gesture of progressive reciprocity need only be sincere and intriguing—you won't be judged on its success in generating specific value. Its purpose is to motivate your critical enabler to help you and in doing so to make it clear that you're not simply another leech trying to get something of value without giving anything in return. You're presenting yourself as someone who wants to earn help through offering your personal resourcefulness and spending time understanding your critical enabler's needs.

How Do You Know What to Offer?

Once you've done your initial general research and gotten an idea of your prospective critical enabler's personality and interests, refine the development of your gesture. The way to do that is by asking a series of specific questions that will help you narrow your focus on a prospective critical enabler:

- What kind of intelligence would help advance your prospect's interests?

- What could your prospect do to find new customers or clients?

- What new markets or territories might your prospect want to penetrate?

- What other companies or businesses serve the same market as your prospect without being competitors?

- What products or services will your prospect's company be competing with in developing its product or service line?

- What weak links in your prospect's supply chain might you be able to help with?

- What profile describes the ideal member or subscriber for your prospect's organization or journal?

- What charitable causes does your prospect support?

- What can you do personally, based on your own background or professional experience, that would be of value to your prospect?

Use these questions as starting points to trigger ideas of how you can develop a gesture that seems likely to turn your prospect into a critical enabler. I think you will be quite surprised how unlocking the limits on your thinking allows you to come up with what might initially have seemed to you to be unlikely sources of reciprocity currency, enabling you to make connections and deliver on your gesture in wonderfully unexpected ways.

Things You Already Know

What kind of intelligence would help advance your prospect's interests?

Intelligence that is useful to your prospective critical enabler is among the first things you might look for when creating a gesture of progressive reciprocity. It doesn't need to be some secret or mysterious information that you have to go undercover to obtain—in fact, real secrets are not appropriate here. I'm talking very generally about potentially useful knowledge that your prospect is likely to perceive as valuable.

Here are some areas you can explore as you develop a gesture of progressive reciprocity based on what you know that your prospect doesn't:

- Intelligence that helps improve your critical enabler's marketing
- Intelligence about your critical enabler's competitors
- Intelligence about technologies that your critical enabler might find useful

- Intelligence about how your critical enabler's product or service is perceived in the marketplace by clients or customers

- Intelligence about trends or anything new that could affect your critical enabler's business

My client Judith gained a marketing boost for her company by capitalizing on the valuable intelligence she could offer to her prospective critical enabler, the CEO of a company in a related field. In her research, she discovered that the company never appeared in Google search results until the third or fourth screen, and that triggered her idea for reciprocity. Judith had been working on revising her own company's Internet marketing plan, and her technical support staff had recently updated the Web site's search engine optimization (SEO) strategy to guarantee top placements when people used search terms relevant to the company's products and services. This seemed to be a likely opening to her prospect, so Judith sent him an introductory e-mail.

In wording her message, Judith was careful to avoid assumptions about her prospect's marketing strategy. She explained that she'd been doing research about the company and had noticed that its Web site generally appeared only quite low in the search results. She wondered if the prospect might be interested in hearing about a new SEO strategy that her own company had developed, and she offered to share it if it was of interest. The prospect was impressed that Judith had taken the time to do this level of research and replied by offering to schedule a meeting.

There are a number of things to avoid, however, as you develop an intelligence-based gesture of progressive reciprocity. First, never offer any proprietary information or information you obtained on condition of not passing it on. In particular, avoid basing your gesture on confidential information about your prospect's competition, including anything you might have gathered when you were working for a competitor. Passing along this type of intelligence ("You didn't hear this from me, but . . .") will almost invariably damage rather than enhance your chances. Your prospect is all too likely to figure you'd probably be as free with information about anyone who trusts you not to disclose it.

Second, avoid gossip. For instance, if you find yourself shaping a comment like, "I heard that the head of R&D over at your competitor is leaving, and I think that means they're going to go in a new direction," stop and regroup. By passing along anything you might have heard around the water cooler but can't document, you're indicating to your critical enabler that your judgment is questionable.

Finally, avoid passing along secondhand social marketing intelligence as a gesture of progressive reciprocity. Especially in this age of Twitter and other rapid-response networking sites, many people reuse links they stumble upon or pass along references to books or articles they haven't read. Sending such messages tags you as someone who hasn't bothered to do real background work, and that will do little or nothing to build a relationship with a prospective critical enabler. Here's the real question to ask yourself as a test: If I were the recipient, would I view this information as uniquely appropriate to my business or situation? You want the recipient to respond, *Wow, this is quite relevant to [my current challenge]!*

Business-Building Tips

What could your prospect do to find new customers or clients?

For many people in a position to serve as critical enablers, especially those who own their own companies or are compensated or awarded bonuses based on the business they write, gestures of progressive reciprocity that identify potential sources of new business are very attractive. This can be even more true if your prospect works for a smaller company of the type that operates on the maxim "everyone sells." The smaller and more early-stage the company, the more likely everyone in the organization will welcome sales leads, even if they're not directly involved in sales themselves. And entrepreneurs simply have to be resourceful about everything, especially about strategic new business development channel partnerships.

As noted earlier, it isn't essential that your gesture of progressive reciprocity actually results in a new sale, deal, revenue source, or business relationship for your prospective critical enabler. In most cases, just the chance of potential new business is enough to persuade a prospect to see your worthiness and be motivated to provide what you are asking for. I remember apologizing to a critical enabler in my own network because none of my eight proposed new business opportunities had materialized. To me it felt a bit like I had cried wolf too many times. Yet this critical enabler quickly reassured me that in his business he expected to kiss thirty frogs before one turned into a princess and that he still greatly appreciated my offers. It turned out that soon thereafter one of my leads did result in a closed deal. The critical enabler came back, profusely appreciative, and made the point that my hit rate had been better than his sales team's—but that was an extra benefit; the gesture of progressive reciprocity had already done its work for me. This organization was uniquely positioned to know and refer qualified clients for my business, which they did, numerous times.

The following real-life examples illustrate more ways to build your business by presenting the right lead.

Finding a Way In

Max, who was looking to change jobs, had identified as his prospective critical enabler a woman who owned a small business that specialized in organizing regional trade show events and conferences targeted at manufacturing companies, and who thus dealt with many of the decision makers he wanted to approach about employment. Because her livelihood depended directly on how many clients her company could serve, she was always looking for new connections.

Max worked for a manufacturing company, and he had already dealt with this woman. He was also very familiar with other manufacturing companies in the region—some were customers, some were vendors, and some were competitors. But he initially told me he thought he couldn't introduce any new clients to her, because she knew everyone in the industry. I replied that although that might be true, she looked like the perfect critical enabler. "You have to at least try to generate a gesture of progressive reciprocity for her!"

Once he set his negative thinking aside, Max researched his prospect's company Web site. He was surprised to notice the absence of several companies that he thought should be listed as attending her conferences and using her services at trade shows—and he knew many of the decision makers at those companies.

In approaching her, Max said, "You know, it occurred to me that you and I are targeting many of the same companies, although for different reasons, and I'm thinking we might be able to collaborate. I think I can give you information that will help you develop client relationships with companies you're not currently working with. And of course, there is no question you could help me because, well . . . you know everyone in my target field." In their first conversation, he offered the name of a specific company that wasn't on her client list, along with the name of the decision maker she needed to contact. He also told her to feel free to use his name when she made use of the referral.

She welcomed the information, and in return she was very willing to share what she knew about the types of companies Max wanted to work for. In fact, her intelligence and her contacts led Max straight to the job he was looking for, while what he provided to her was of great value in building her business.

Making New Ties

Richard was looking to expand the market for his company's accelerometers—electronic motion-detecting devices that were embedded in many other companies' products, including cameras, GPS units, and mobile phones. He'd identified as his prospective critical enabler the head of engineering for a manufacturer of mobile heart defibrillators, another product in which his company's accelerometers were used. Richard was certain that his prospect could help him identify other potential customers for his company's devices.

Richard had worked with his prospect before, and he was somewhat knowledgeable about his prospect's marketing efforts. These focused on businesses such as airlines, ambulance services, and bus companies that need to be prepared with emergency equipment in case any of their passengers suffer a heart attack. Richard also knew that the company was expanding its marketing to include businesses such as gyms and other recreation facilities. In reviewing his network, Richard recalled a business acquaintance who was a partner in a company that was investing in the health and fitness industry, specifically in acquiring gyms. He called the acquaintance and asked if he'd be interested in receiving a presentation about defibrillation devices from his prospect.

After receiving a go-ahead, Richard approached his prospect. He mentioned that he thought the prospect might be able to help him develop contacts with other companies that could use his own company's accelerometers in their products, but that he first wanted to set up a meeting between the prospect and his business acquaintance to explore a lead into a market the company hadn't fully penetrated. The prospect happily served as a critical enabler for Richard, providing exactly the referrals to contacts in other industries and the information about them that he needed to expand his company's business.

Breaking into Government

Celeste owned a small company that produced and packaged "green energy" solutions for businesses. She was interested in marketing her company's services to state and municipal government offices, and she'd identified a partner at an executive search firm as a critical enabler who specialized in and could easily put her in contact with decision makers at agencies that would be potential customers.

But Celeste expressed a valid objection about this critical enabler. "Of course this headhunter is the perfect critical enabler for me because of her business and networks," she said. "And I know I'm not the only one thinking the same thing. These search guys and gals are constantly getting hit up for referrals to their networks. Plus, making referrals is essentially what they get paid to do. So why would this one help me in the way that I need?"

"Let's just see about that," I said. So we discussed the fact that recruiting firms, especially these days, were always looking for new search assignments. And of course, out-of-work executives outnumbered the places available in companies that might pay for the firm's placement services. Celeste knew of a small company that was on a rapid growth trajectory and might be interested in the executive placement company's services, and she called her prospect with an offer to put her in contact with the president of this growing company.

"That's a pleasant surprise," the prospect replied. "Nobody ever calls us to offer new clients. The only thing they want is for us to help them find jobs."

Celeste explained that although she did know that her friend's company was hiring, she couldn't guarantee that it would be able to justify paying a search fee to find talent. She did think, though, that it might use her prospect's services, and that was the key to the success of the exchange. Subsequently, the prospect was happy to provide referrals to several key regional government officials likely to be willing to meet with Celeste in exchange for the potential source of new business for her company.

Expansion Ideas

What new markets or territories might your prospect want to penetrate?

You can help your prospective critical enabler's business expand by identifying fresh areas that it could serve. To do this, think of new applications for its existing products or services—ways they might be repurposed to serve a different or expanded market, or existing products from other organizations that they might integrate with to reach new areas of the market.

Also look at other services or products that are consumed along with or used in conjunction with those of your critical enabler. Think in terms of "co-branding"—combining your prospect's products or services with those of another company to create a new hybrid offering. This is often one of the most productive areas to explore in developing your gesture of progressive reciprocity, and in many cases you'll find that you already have the reciprocity currency you need to make an intriguing offer.

Three of my clients used the power of expansion opportunities to broker new relationships (including their own).

Cleanliness Is Next to Success

Jonathan worked for a struggling business publication that desperately needed an award-winning story to boost subscription sales. His boss was pressuring him to get something out much faster than normal to come out alongside an upcoming FDA ruling (even though "normal" speed in his business was insanely aggressive to begin with). Jonathan's goal was to write the definitive work about cutting-edge antimicrobial technology and applications, a field he wasn't that familiar with. He needed to find and befriend one industry authority who not only could tell him everything he needed to know for the story but also would be willing to share some fairly proprietary knowledge with him. And he needed to do this fast. This urgency led Jonathan to approach the head of engineering at a company that specialized in using silver (a powerful antimicrobial agent) as the basis for products that helped prevent the spread of germs and that therefore actively sought partners in whose products its antimicrobial technology could be incorporated.

Jonathan was an avid practitioner of yoga. From personal experience and observation, he knew that yoga enthusiasts generally don't like carrying their own mats and other equipment around with them, but they like even less the thought of using equipment that's been used by other people. In other words, sanitation is a key issue.

Through writing other health-related stories, Jonathan had developed relationships with a number of manufacturers of yoga-related products, including yoga mats, bands used in stretching, and other yoga accessories. When he was looking for a way to develop a gesture of progressive reciprocity for this silver technology company's head of engineering, Jonathan saw that helping the company penetrate a new market would be the ideal way to make that happen. He mentioned to his friend that using his critical enabler's technology to permanently sanitize yoga equipment would be an excellent way to add value to his products, and the friend loved the idea. In approaching his prospect, Jonathan offered to put him in touch with his friend at the yoga accessories manufacturing company, making him feel much better about asking for the research he needed for what turned out to be his award-winning story. The gesture was greatly appreciated by both of the people he brought together—a real win-win-win situation.

Building Security

Sandra had recently taken a job as vice president of business development for a network security company. The company provided consulting services that focused on keeping corporate data secure—in effect, bulletproofing clients' data. One of the market segments it focused on was financial institutions, including banks and credit card companies. Sandra was looking to develop a client base of businesses with extensive information assets and IT operations, for whom security was a particularly important concern.

Sandra had identified a company that specialized in providing data storage solutions for corporate clients as a likely place to find a critical enabler, and she'd gotten a referral to a former vice president of the company who had recently left that position to form his own data storage firm. Just like Sandra's, the new company was competing with larger rivals for clients, and both were attempting to build their portfolios rapidly.

Sandra's e-mail to her prospective critical enabler emphasized the fact that their companies served similar markets with different but complementary products. She also mentioned two clients to whom she would be happy to provide referrals, and she suggested that she and her prospect meet to discuss putting together an informal partnership, with each asking their clients about the needs and challenges the other's services addressed. By actively keeping an eye out for each other, they both enjoyed a flurry of cross-referrals and a spike in revenue.

Pinpoint Location

Samuel had a company based on software that could capture GPS data from police patrol cars and analyze it to show the best possible routes—the ones that would provide optimal patrol car coverage in large cities. He had identified a potential critical enabler who worked for a large company that provided communications support to all of his state's police departments. He wanted to convince his prospect to refer him to police departments that might be interested in GPS-processing software.

One of Samuel's friends was marketing an application that let homeowners monitor energy consumption in their houses and display dynamic presentations of their energy usage on their television screens. Samuel immediately recognized that this technology might be a perfect complement to the technology of the prospect he was approaching, and he got the OK from his friend to mention his company to his prospective critical enabler. In his initial phone call, Samuel told his prospect about his friend's company and said he thought it might be a good fit with the cable TV and Internet services that the critical enabler's company provided. Samuel also explained that his own company had developed new technology that could be very useful to police departments in tracking patrol car activity, and that he wanted to get referrals to police departments around the state to pitch the product. The communications executive was happy to provide referrals to Samuel in exchange for the lead on the complementary technology developed by his friend's company.

Potential Alliance Partners

What other companies or businesses serve the same market as your prospect's without being competitors?

To implement another effective strategy, examine the market your prospective critical enabler's company competes in. Companies that serve the same customer base with unrelated products are natural allies. For instance, suppliers of nutritional supplements serve the same market as personal trainers: people committed to their own personal fitness. Likewise, a day care service works in the same market as a dog walker: busy people who need help taking care of those whose welfare is their responsibility. Many mutually beneficial relationships have been forged based on building connections between companies that serve the same market with different products or services.

Here are two more individuals who each identified and developed partnerships of mutual support that paid off handsomely for all concerned.

Finding a Buyer

Julie had built up a small natural foods production company, and now she was ready to sell it. For a critical enabler, she was looking into a food distribution company that handled products for many of the companies she regarded as potential buyers. Her research into this distributor revealed that its client list omitted several manufacturers with whom she had ongoing relationships.

Julie approached the distributor's CEO with an offer to provide referrals to these companies, and she mentioned her interest in referrals to the decision makers in companies that might be interested in purchasing her business.

The CEO immediately welcomed the opportunity to expand his own business. And although he wasn't a distributor for Julie's products, he knew of the company and its excellent reputation, and he had no qualms about recommending Julie to a possible acquirer he knew. In exchange for referrals to a number of manufacturers that might use his distribution service, he identified the ideal candidate to purchase Julie's brand: a regional food manufacturer that was expanding by buying up smaller companies.

The relationship eventually resulted in two positive outcomes: the distributor was able to pick up distribution for two large manufacturers that wanted to sell their products in his region, and Julie was able to sell her company to the one the distributor had recommended to her.

Finding Patients

Perry, a psychiatrist who specialized in behavioral disorders, was looking for more patients. He identified a prospective critical enabler whose company had developed a diagnostic monitor that tracked the activity of children with behavioral disorders and pinpointed the specific disorder that their activity patterns indicated they had. Perry felt that this prospect would be an excellent source of patient referrals for his psychiatry practice.

One of Perry's business acquaintances had developed a new and highly effective treatment for people suffering from post-traumatic stress disorder (PTSD), and Perry wanted to bring him together with his prospect. Perry reasoned that it would benefit his prospect by enabling him to refer his clients suffering from PTSD to someone who'd developed an effective treatment. His business acquaintance thought it would be a great idea, and Perry proposed it as a gesture of progressive reciprocity to his prospect, who also liked the sound of it. In the end, Perry gained a new source of patient referrals for his practice while bringing together two people who served the same market with complementary services.

News of the Competition

What products or services will your prospect's company be competing with in developing its product or service line?

Surprisingly often, people who would be ideal critical enablers are too busy marketing their own company's products or services to have the time to do a good competitive analysis. Meanwhile, if you're interested in that industry, you're likely spending a lot of time and energy collecting information about it. What you want, of course, is the information and intelligence you need to fulfill your own business objective, and you may feel like you're spinning your wheels until you find exactly what you're looking for. But don't undervalue those efforts—information that is useless for your primary purpose may well be useful to someone else. You can repurpose it fairly easily into competitive intelligence that makes an effective gesture of progressive reciprocity for your prospect.

It helps to realize that you don't have to have an entire competitive report to offer for it to be of value. Something as simple as a tip you picked up about a prospect's competitors being considered as an acquisition by XYZ Co. is valuable—just make sure you didn't pick it up under conditions that make it confidential information.

My client Megan was head of R&D at a genetic engineering company ("genco") charged with developing a new cancer treatment product. The problem was that her industry is very fragmented, with thousands of companies scattered around the globe, many of them quite small and low profile and all working on different products. There's often a great deal of duplication of effort among the companies involved in this type of research and development, and Megan felt she desperately needed intelligence about what other developers might be about to deliver.

Megan needed a reliable source of information on what other companies were working on. She'd identified several potential sources that maintained databases that tracked developments in genomics and genetic engineering. One looked like a particularly good source for the information she needed, but it sold the data it developed at prices Megan's budget didn't cover. When she began to examine the gestures of progressive reciprocity she might make in her approach to a prospective critical enabler there, she focused on the fact that the database company was in a market as competitive as her own.

Megan realized the information about all of the other genomics data companies (the ones she either didn't like or also couldn't afford) could be useful to the company whose database she really wanted. When she approached her prospect, she asked whether the spreadsheet she'd developed for comparing all the genco competitors for her own purposes would be interesting. The prospect was intrigued enough to set up a meeting, and eventually arranged for her to acquire the information she needed at a substantial discount.

Forging Links in a Chain

What weak links in your prospect's supply chain might you be able to help with?

In answering this question, picture your critical enabler's business as a web of chains linked with customers, suppliers, service vendors, distributors, or resellers. Each of these links is a possible place for a gesture of progressive reciprocity. That leads to the next question: "Is there any knowledge or relationship I or someone in my network might have in these areas that I can develop for my critical enabler?"

By scoping the market, two of my clients found ways to forge links with critical enablers and others to which they were linked.

Getting a Foot in the Door

Terrence had just relocated from the West Coast to the East Coast and was looking for a job with a sporting goods apparel manufacturer similar to the one he'd left. He'd applied for a job with a company that made athletic shoes, and although it turned out the company was not hiring, he realized that its CEO must know everyone in her industry in the area and surely had the intelligence he needed, making her an ideal critical enabler. Terrence decided to take advantage of his knowledge of outsourcing footwear manufacturing to develop a gesture of progressive reciprocity. He e-mailed his prospect explaining that he had done some investigation about her company after he'd become familiar with its footwear line and had found a manufacturer that seemed likely to save her company a significant amount of money. He included the manufacturer's costs for products similar to some of those her company was producing.

She picked up the phone and called Terrence, saying she'd very much like to discuss the information he'd sent her, which seemed likely to save her upward of a million dollars annually. Then, without any prompting from Terrence, she asked what she might do for him in return. Terrence was able to help his critical enabler find a new manufacturer for one of her product lines, and she in return provided him with referrals and intelligence about companies she thought would be looking to hire someone with his capabilities.

Switching Industries

Gregg was an industrial engineer in the process of moving to the financial services industry, and he had identified a prospective critical enabler at a large organization in his new field. He had a personal account with his prospect's company, which put him in a position to observe what he described as "serious continuity problems" with the reports he received. He inferred that the back-office processing was inefficient at capturing, monitoring, and updating customer information, so clients were not receiving their statements on time. In addition, it was clear that the reports were not generated centrally; instead, each type of report was produced independently by different departments or personnel, all working by hand and without necessarily having access to the same data.

Gregg approached his prospect by explaining that he knew thought leaders who had helped a major company develop efficiencies in manufacturing processes, and he reasoned that his prospect's company, even though it was not a manufacturing operation, might benefit from a consultation about best practices with the engineers he was referring to. He gave his prospect a referral to one of his contacts, and the response was immediately positive. His prospect recognized that his firm had supply chain problems, and the firm ended up adopting many of the recommendations of the manufacturing engineers that Gregg referred to them. Prompted by his gesture of progressive reciprocity, Gregg received referrals to several people in the financial industry likely to be interested in hiring him.

Membership Leads

What profile describes the ideal member or subscriber for your prospect's organization or journal?

Professional organizations are among the best, most efficient, and most *under*utilized places to find critical enabler thought leaders when you're developing a gesture of progressive reciprocity. Membership directors of these organizations tend to gravitate toward their jobs because they're excellent networkers, and, as part of their job responsibilities, they tend to develop their networks very fully. Further, their job is to increase membership rolls, so they almost always welcome help with that task. Program directors of professional organizations also tend to be excellent sources of intelligence, because they work directly with industry thought leaders to develop the content of presentations and activities to retain members and attract new members.

My clients Sarah and Jerry did their homework to build background information that provided valuable progressive reciprocity for their potential critical enablers.

Getting Up to Speed

Sarah wanted to make a diagonal move in her company, going from quality assurance to the product development division. She needed to quickly develop information on the new area. Sarah had identified the membership director of a leading professional association in her field as someone likely to direct her to the thought leaders from whom she could gather the information she needed to make the transition.

As part of her research into her prospective critical enabler's needs, Sarah searched through her network looking for contacts who might be able to help her prospect find new members. Her old department at the university she'd graduated from might be an excellent source of leads, she thought. She decided to suggest that her prospect and the department head—with whom she had worked to develop her undergraduate thesis—could develop a relationship that would likely be beneficial to both.

Sarah contacted her thesis adviser, mentioning that she would be approaching the membership director and that she thought it might be beneficial for his department and the professional organization to develop a relationship.

Her professor liked the idea very much—he had already identified improving the department's outreach efforts as something he needed to do—and he gave her the go-ahead to arrange a meeting.

In her initial phone call to her prospect, Sarah began by saying that her old thesis adviser liked the idea of referring potential new members to the organization, feeling the university would gain from such a relationship—especially in the area of enabling its students to make valuable contacts as they were preparing to go out into the business world. Sarah went so far as to suggest they might set up a model program based on her prospect's organization working with colleges and universities in this way.

Sarah then explained that she herself was interested in talking with several industry thought leaders in order to gain the intelligence she needed to move into a new area within her company. Her prospect welcomed the opportunity to help, and he agreed to refer Sarah to several people from whom she could gain the information she was seeking. Her strategy was such a success that she soon found her ideal job—and in making the offer, her new department head made it a point to note that she had distinguished herself from other applicants for the job by the depth and breadth of knowledge she demonstrated about the company's products and those of its competitors in the industry.

Finding a Connection

Jerry wanted to interview for the job of vice president of marketing that had just opened up at a major corporation, so he was seeking a referral to the person in charge of hiring for that position. On one of the social networking sites he frequented, he discovered that someone in his network—a man he'd met casually about a year earlier—had a direct connection to the person he wanted to meet. He didn't know the network member well enough to just call him and ask for a referral, so we began to search for a gesture of progressive reciprocity Jerry could make to turn this remote connection into a critical enabler.

In gathering background information on the prospect, we noted that he worked for a customer loyalty analytics company that was in the business of researching and analyzing customer franchises. The subscriber profile for the company's services included businesses that kept very close tabs on their customers and clients, and when Jerry discovered that, the light went on. Earlier in his career, Jerry had worked for an international magazine that was constantly looking for ways to capture feedback about its readers' satisfaction with the product. The magazine was the most subscriber-oriented business he could imagine, and he felt it would be a perfect candidate to use his critical enabler's services as a way of getting insight into its customers.

Jerry approached his prospect with an offer to refer him to a decision maker at the magazine he used to work for; in exchange, he requested a referral to the decision maker in charge of hiring for the position he was seeking. The critical enabler was happy to exchange referrals, commenting that the magazine Jerry had recommended seemed to be an ideal candidate for his company's services.

Common Ground

What charitable causes does your prospect support?

Many people pride themselves on their commitment to community service, and this can be a productive area to examine as you develop your gesture of progressive reciprocity. Find the names of specific charities or nonprofits your critical enabler is associated with and explore the possibility of helping support their activity.

If you look beyond business connections and consider other aspects of life, you're apt to find your prospect's true passions. This kind of information is often easy to find on social networking sites. If you're on the same journey in some level of "real life"—that is, outside of business—you may find a gesture of progressive reciprocity that really matters to your prospect.

My client Colleen was preparing her company for an IPO, and she had identified the managing director of an investment bank as a prospective critical enabler who could help her work through the details of the exit strategy to be included in her business plan. As we researched her prospect's interests, we discovered that he was very involved with a nonprofit organization that ran homeless shelters. When I suggested that we explore this further, Colleen demurred, saying that she couldn't imagine what she could provide that would be of benefit to this charitable organization.

I suggested that despite her reservations we continue to explore this area, starting with the question, "What do homeless shelters need?"

"Well, food, of course," Colleen said, adding that homeless shelters are basically in the business of providing meals for their clients. This triggered an interesting connection. Colleen recalled that she had a friend who owned a turkey farm, and turkeys were certainly something a homeless shelter could use in almost endless quantity. She immediately called her friend to ask whether he'd be interested in making a donation of frozen turkeys to the homeless shelters her critical enabler was affiliated with. Her friend, recognizing the opportunity to provide a valuable service that would also generate good publicity, said he would do so.

When Colleen's prospect learned of the offer of holiday turkeys, he was delighted, saying that he couldn't wait to let others at the shelters know of the donation. In return, the bank officer was more than willing to help Colleen develop her exit strategy. The result was an ongoing relationship in which Colleen's friend provided the homeless shelters with annual donations of turkeys for the Thanksgiving and Christmas holidays. Colleen, in turn, was able to complete her public offering while paying significantly lower investment bank fees.

Things You Can Do

What can you do personally, based on your own background or professional experience, that would be of value to your prospect?

When you're preparing to approach the people who have the information and contacts you need, you often need to use lateral thinking. Rather than asking individuals for the information you want, for example, you can poll a discussion forum on a topic of general interest and offer to share the collective response to those who participate—that's a fairly easy way of creating quick value. Or you can post a survey, article, or even a white paper about best practices and then approach a variety of people who'd be good critical enablers (along with other industry leaders) and offer the opportunity to contribute to it and be quoted in your write-up.

Although this might seem like a lot of extra work just to persuade someone to provide referrals and information, it can be a strategic move. I've worked with a number of people who were breaking into totally new fields and took this tack. They gained not only access to critical enablers but also instant credibility, simply by virtue of collecting and posting thought leaders' questions and answers about an important but underaddressed issue in the field. It is kind of like being a reporter. The real story or value comes from the interviewees, but just by association the person preparing the report becomes regarded as a valuable resource—someone deserving of further help. That's certainly what my client Mary discovered.

Mary wanted to get back to consulting now that her children were in school. Because of her own medical history and her experience with overseeing her young children's medical care and that of her aging parents, she had developed a special interest in applying her expertise in the medical industry, where she was certain her skills could make a big difference in changing industry standards and best practices for the better.

Mary had identified several prospective critical enablers, including one hospital chief medical officer who was scheduled to give a talk at a convention in a city near where she lived. It was too late to set up a meeting or even to query her network and see if she could get an introduction, so she determined that she would attend his lecture and approach him directly with her proposal. Mary attended the conference, and she was the first in line to speak with her contact after his talk. After introducing herself, she made her gesture of progressive reciprocity very directly by saying, "I'm working on a white paper about what key medical industry executives think are the most important best-practices issues that need to be addressed today, and I'd very much like to get your input on the subject."

Her contact responded immediately and positively, saying that he'd be honored to help her out. He shared his contact information with her and suggested she call his administrative assistant to set up an interview. During the interview, her critical enabler not only answered her questions about which issues he felt were currently most important, but also made suggestions as to how such a survey might be worded, and he suggested she use his name to contact two other people he was sure would want to contribute to her project.

Mary's gesture of progressive reciprocity was proposing that her critical enabler work with her to develop a paper that would very likely be of great benefit to the entire medical industry. She was giving him and others she approached a chance to give back to their industry. In the process, she discovered that she was able to obtain not only an interview with one industry leader but access to other industry leaders as well, dramatically expanding her pool of critical enablers.

After her interviews with the two referrals that her initial critical enabler had provided, word of Mary's project began to spread quite rapidly. She found she no longer needed to try to find a job; rather, the jobs were trying to find her. Within the next two months, she had no fewer than three offers from consulting firms that worked in her target field, and she also was approached by two hospitals that wanted to hire her to work on implementing organizational changes based on correcting best-practices issues they had identified.

What Else Can You Try?

What if you can't find the right gesture of progressive reciprocity in your initial research about your prospect?

It sometimes happens that you don't hit on precisely the right gesture to establish the kind or level of progressive reciprocity that you would like. Your initial offer may not be something your prospective critical enabler actually values, or you simply may not be able to discover a sufficiently compelling gesture. In that case, don't just abandon the idea; before you go back to square one and look for another person who could serve as your critical enabler, rethink and redefine your approach to your first choice.

If you can arrange a meeting, focus it on your prospect. That is, turn it into a sort of needs interview, an in-person getting-to-know-you meeting in which you follow up to find more information about what's important to your critical enabler and how you might use that knowledge to make a meaningful gesture of progressive reciprocity. Look for information about what the prospect does and what factors affect the prospect's performance appraisal, along with markets the prospect wants to reach and activities the prospect engages in outside business. Chances are that this discussion will suggest a gesture of progressive reciprocity you can make on the spot or in the future.

Although you may initially find that your prospective critical enabler is reluctant to reveal any real needs, continue to diplomatically and respectfully probe this area, because you never know where your critical enabler's need is going to pop up. Even if you ultimately can't deliver a gesture of progressive reciprocity, your efforts to do so will not go unnoticed. You'll gain a great deal of respect from your critical enabler for your efforts, because you made it clear how important such gestures are to you. I liken it to a math test in which, even if you can't come up with the right answer, you get points for "showing your work."

In my experience this does work almost all of the time. If you look for a connection that allows you to offer something your prospect finds valuable, or at least meaningful enough to give you credit for trying, you can almost always find one. In my experience, even the people who are toughest to get anything from are softened by this approach—to the point of providing things they normally would never even consider. So don't give up or give in to early pessimism; the gesture of progressive reciprocity really is almost uniformly effective—as my persevering client Aaron learned.

Aaron was trying to build a leadership consulting practice, so I referred him to a well-known thought leader whose own consulting practice focused on leadership transitions; I thought he would be ideal as a critical enabler for Aaron's quest for clients. The two were consulting with the same kinds of clients but were taking different approaches by focusing on different aspects of corporate transition consulting.

Aaron's original gesture of progressive reciprocity was an offer to refer his critical enabler to a corporate client with whom he was currently working. Although his critical enabler had agreed to an initial meeting, Aaron was concerned that he hadn't really found the right gesture and that his approach might not get him the results he wanted.

Aaron's worries were confirmed early in their first meeting, when his critical enabler danced around the specifics of what their business relationship might involve. It was clear that something more was needed, and Aaron determined to find a better, more compelling offer. To do that, he continued to ask his critical enabler questions and to exchange information with him about various topics, including business objectives and methods as well as personal history. When they got around to talking about their upcoming summer plans, Aaron learned that his prospect was planning a trip to France with his family, including a chartered barge up the Seine River into Belgium. As it turned out, Aaron had a wealth of reciprocity currency he'd no idea he possessed.

It so happened that Aaron had vacationed in France with his family and they had taken several trips up the Seine—precisely the same type of trip his prospect was planning. Aaron had found that the primary key to making such a trip pleasant and relaxing was finding the right captain for the charter. In his travels, Aaron had acquired a great deal of knowledge about the captains in the business, and he was able to say, "Here's the captain you need to call. He's the best and most reliable and least expensive out of dozens I've met or heard of." The prospect immediately responded by saying, "You don't know how much this means to me. My wife has been after me to work on this part of our trip, and I didn't know where to begin to research it, and I wouldn't have the time even if I did." Then he said, "Now, what was it you were looking for?"

In many cases you simply can't know in advance what reciprocity currency you might be able to call on with your potential critical enabler. Aaron achieved his goal by becoming a critical enabler in the very specialized and somewhat obscure area of chartered boat trips up the Seine in France for the very person he had identified as his critical enabler!

Continue to try to connect with your critical enablers, to find out who they are on a personal level. This kind of effort to discover who your potential critical enablers are and what they need is another key to unlocking relationships in which true value exchanges can occur.

But not everyone who *can* help *will* help, and eventually it's time to move on. If it doesn't work out after your own best efforts, simply look for another prospect—as discussed in Chapter Seven.

What Do You Have to Offer?

Of course, I haven't begun to cover the countless business situations you might become involved in. If none of the questions here apply to your particular case, develop your own. Use the questions and stories in this chapter as models to expand your own exploration of your reciprocity currency.

Many people find themselves by default spending their time online engaging in unproductive digital networking activities rather than making targeted requests for assistance. The reason often boils down to a somewhat distorted mental image: when they imagine actually asking people for something, whether it's a job or funding or any other business favor, they see themselves as down on their knees begging. They see themselves as submissive, not in control, in the weak position of having to ask.

When you offer a gesture of progressive reciprocity, you reverse that equation. You become the one in control, the one offering help—and it's remarkable how empowering such a gesture is. It levels the playing field, essentially reframing the important issues, changing the focus from approaching your critical enabler asking for help to offering something of value in advance. And once you begin the practice of offering something in advance before you ask for something for yourself, you'll discover that it's much easier to approach people. You'll be able to honestly say that you have the express intent of helping your critical enabler, and you'll find that is an enormous confidence-booster.

CHAPTER 7

The Right Person

SELECTING A CRITICAL ENABLER WHO IS
INCLINED, AVAILABLE, AND LIKE-MINDED

*Gordon (yeah, his last name is Curtis) wanted to produce
a book outlining his insights into the pursuit of business
objectives. He'd never had a book published before, and he
had no connections with agents and no experience in the
process.*

*Applying his own system, he decided he needed a
critical enabler to help him find and meet the right agent.
After some thought, he concluded that he would find the
knowledge he needed among people working in the industry
or providing services to it, such as attorneys working on
publishing and intellectual property issues.*

*He got in touch with the half-dozen trusted advisers in
his network who were in fields somehow related to publishing to ask whether they knew anyone in these categories.
This netted him three names—one man who ran a printing
company and two attorneys—and he studied their backgrounds and interests to see which were likely to help him.*

*The printer looked like the best prospect, especially
when Gordon checked LinkedIn and discovered a mutual*

connection he could call on—and then realized that he might actually have met the printer himself long ago, if they'd been members of the same swim team as children. Jackpot, he thought. He phoned the connection—a childhood friend—to confirm that the printer was the one he remembered and to get the friend's permission to mention him when talking about old times. The friend agreed, so he had the referral nailed down. He also came up with a tasty gesture of progressive reciprocity—an introduction to another connection who had developed an interesting short-run printing technology. And first contact seemed promising. They had a pleasant preliminary conversation, and the printer expressed interest and said he'd think about possibilities. Gordon followed up with a promised e-mail, but nothing happened, nor did he get a response when he phoned. Gordon finally realized the printer just wasn't going to help him.

Despite the apparent line-up, it had become clear that the printer really wasn't inclined or available to act as a critical enabler for the book project. So Gordon chalked that effort up to experience, and he returned to his list of prospects. One of the attorneys on the list seemed a pretty remote possibility—the trusted adviser who mentioned him said she wasn't even sure he'd remember her name—but when asked if he seemed like someone who'd be approachable, she cheerfully confirmed it. A review of background information showed that the man had taught sociology before becoming an attorney, and he maintained an interest in social science and is a former psychology professor at Harvard and Brandeis—he looked like a perfect match for a *social networking book. Besides, as a gesture of progressive reciprocity, Gordon could offer a referral to someone in his network who might need advice on publishing law.*

His new prospective critical enabler responded to Gordon's e-mail within the hour, offering a referral to the agent who wound up placing this book with Jossey-Bass.

Possessing the knowledge you need isn't enough to make someone an effective critical enabler, and sometimes even the best-chosen gesture of progressive reciprocity won't turn reluctance into support. Up to this point, I've been discussing three of the elements of a blockbuster introduction as though they will always work. And indeed it's true that you have to find someone *knowledgeable*—with the right information and contacts—and you have to set things up so your prospect will feel both *obligated* and *motivated* to help you; thus these three basics:

- *Knowledgeable:* Successful networkers know what they want, and they talk to contacts who have the exact knowledge or relationships they need.

- *Obligated:* Successful requests for assistance happen when the contact feels an obligation based on a referral or some previous association with the networker.

- *Motivated:* Successful requests for assistance require something in addition to a sense of obligation; the networker still needs to offer the contact a reason to go out of the way to help, to stimulate their willingness to help.

But to be sure you have the right person, you need to look beyond these three elements. In particular, you want to look for someone who is

- *Inclined:* Successful meetings happen with contacts who understand the value of, and enjoy, investing time in helping other people.

- *Available:* Successful connections require the follow-through to deliver—not just a promise to do so that never translates into finding time for a meeting.

- *Like-minded:* Successful exchanges begin with a real connection—some commonality between the networker and the contact.

The more of these factors you can bring to bear, the higher the likelihood that your contact with a prospective critical enabler will be successful. And when you have all of them, I can predict with certainty that the outcome of your encounter will be blockbuster.

What Makes Someone the Right Person?

The three characteristics that make a prospective critical enabler with the requisite knowledge virtually certain to work out for you are *inclination, availability*, and *like-mindedness.* Although I've seen many Right Person–Right Approach relationships succeed without some of these qualities, those that turned out to be truly blockbuster in terms of mutual benefit and exchange possessed these characteristics. Hence, it's best to look for a prospect who possesses them all.

Monitoring these qualities is the last element of maintaining control over the process. Such qualities generally are fixed in someone else and largely out of your hands, except to the extent that a truly well-chosen gesture of progressive reciprocity can evoke inclination in someone who initially appears to lack it, so your "control" in this area will tend to take the form of choosing which prospects to develop. That is, although these qualities are inherent in the person you are preparing to engage, the control is all yours when it comes to building on them for an easy and productive exchange.

When screening your prospects, prioritize them according to where they fall on the spectrum for each of these characteristics, from zilch to wild abundance. Because your ability to influence these three aspects of personality is so limited, you need to pay attention to them so as to avoid wasting your time and effort on someone who shows signs of disinclination to help you, no matter how attractive the knowledge and relationships they may have.

Inclination

The quality of *inclination* depends mainly on someone's character, and evaluating it can feel more like going by instinct than making a logical assessment. In reviewing your pool of potential critical enablers, it helps to look for people who "feel right"—who seem to have an exceedingly receptive personality type, perhaps backed up by choice of profession, indicative of a natural inclination to be helpful.

If you'd like a more concrete list of qualities to back up your instincts, consider the kinds of people Malcolm Gladwell identifies in *The Tipping Point* as the ones at the heart of getting things done: the connectors who have "a special gift for bringing the world together," and the mavens who want to "solve other people's problems."

The concept of inclination in the Right Person–Right Approach framework builds on the types of people Gladwell describes—the ones "who link us up with the world." However, it is easy to be so dazzled by someone who is well connected that you spend an inordinate amount of time trying to get to know or get a referral from the person, to no avail. But why wouldn't someone who connects with the world connect with you, too? Because connectors are not all created equal, and they're not all disposed to help you in the same way. Some people are connected to a lot of others simply because they are rich or powerful. If so, their connections may largely come to them, and you need to be offering far more than the sort of hopeful gesture that is usually effective if you want to join their crowd.

This view of inclination also builds on the concept of super-connectors Keith Ferrazzi describes in his excellent best-selling book *Never Eat Alone*. These too are the people most likely to be inclined to help. Although they are the ones to look for in your pool of potential critical enablers, however, it is a good idea to look closely to make absolutely sure your time is well spent. Although there are no hard-and-fast rules, here are some clues for spotting people who are likely to be inclined to help you:

- Look at professions where people are paid, rewarded, or even just valued for networking. For example, entrepreneurs, consultants, attorneys, and financial advisers tend to be willing to offer their assistance as critical enablers.

- Look for people who work in relatively small firms, because they can be more likely than people in large firms to have a hand in developing business and are thus required to be more resourceful with their networks. This makes them inclined to be active networkers—and to see you as a potential source of future benefit.

- Look for people whose associates regard them as good connectors. That may seem circular, but it's something you can find out if you ask. That is, when discussing a referral to a potential critical enabler, simply ask, "How approachable is this person? Do you consider him/her a real networker or connector?" It's unlikely that it would occur to anyone to volunteer this kind of information, but almost everyone will know what you are asking.

- And perhaps most important, look at the responses you get. How someone behaves in responding (or not responding) to your first inquiry can tell you a lot about their inclination if you are paying attention.

The key here is to avoid falling into the trap of investing too much time cultivating relationships with people just because they have knowledge and relationships you'd like to tap into. You may not be able to tell who's inclined to help you until you offer a gesture of progressive reciprocity. But if you don't get a positive response and your target either shows no interest in the sort of "needs interview" described in Chapter Six or talks to you without revealing needs you might fill, it may well be time to cut your losses. And even when someone does respond positively to a gesture of progressive reciprocity, you still need to watch carefully for signs of continuing inclination.

Let's look at another client example. Bella looked carefully for inclination in her prospective critical enablers, and she confirmed that this was a make-or-break quality.

Bella had a new job as senior VP of customer service for a company that managed assisted-living facilities. Her first priority was to give the company a clear picture of the amenities it needed to invest in to make its properties more competitive in the marketplace.

Assembling such a picture required significant knowledge about the assisted-living industry—knowledge that Bella, whose prior experience was all in banking, realized she needed to acquire very quickly, both to do her job properly and to avoid discrediting the family friend who'd helped her get it. Like many others facing such a major challenge, she also realized that she couldn't expect on-the-job training. She owed it to her employer to find other ways to come up to speed.

One of the problems was that she was so new to the industry that she didn't know what she didn't know. That became her first focus: how to determine not only what she needed to know but also how and from whom she could acquire that knowledge. Through our discussions she learned she needed to talk to experts in several areas: assisted-living real estate and property management, asset management, and trends in aging. As usual, the key question boiled down to, *Who makes it their business to know what I need to know?*

She shifted to looking for a gatekeeper, a lightning rod, a clearinghouse, or a manager of a watering hole. In her case it soon became evident that it would be someone running a university's center or institute on aging and for someone else who worked in an industry that developed and sold technology to assisted-living facilities. One of the people in her network was a prominent M.D., a family friend who specialized in geriatrics. She went to him and asked whether he could help her by recommending thought leaders in this area to talk to. In addition, she went to the Web site of an assisted-living industry professional association and found blurbs for several conferences that included the professional qualifications of the speakers, and she identified several possible critical enablers in this way.

She narrowed her choice down to two people who likely possessed the knowledge and relationships she knew could catapult her learning curve: a member of the board of directors of an assisted-living professional association who was also a professor of business at a prominent university, and the head of marketing at a health monitoring device company that sold to the assisted-living market. Either of the two seemed likely to have all the knowledge Bella needed to get off to a fast start.

Bella had already done a good deal of research into the industry in her efforts to become familiar with her new territory. For the college professor who was her first prospect, her gesture of progressive reciprocity involved an offer to share the research findings she had collected. That research would, she reasoned, be particularly helpful to him in his specialty field of commercial real estate, and she added an offer to make a presentation to one or more of his classes about the assisted-living real estate market—and to consider his students for internships in her company, which was an industry leader.

Although he agreed to meet with her, he seemed hesitant. "Despite the gesture we came up with, he still made me feel like I was imposing on him by asking him to meet with me," she told me. He opened the meeting by demanding, "How much time will you need from me?" She assured him that she'd be very quick and to the point, but that didn't allay his worries. He was terse, cold, and aloof, and he seemed to think she was asking him for a big favor. These were all indicators that he was not *inclined* to help her, even though she could have offered many things of value to him. She later said ruefully that she knew her normal pit-bullish nature would have led her to keep her jaws locked on this guy as she tried to shake loose the value that appeared so close. However, once she started thinking in terms of inclination, she saw that no matter what she offered, he was not going to open up to her, so she thanked him for his time and departed.

She turned to her second prospect, the marketing director, realizing in hindsight that she probably should have started with him. Prior to taking his current position, he had been head of development (that is, fundraising) for a university, and both that job and his current one were the type that attract strong networkers, people who cultivate many business contacts. She also had a stronger gesture of progressive reciprocity to offer to this prospect:

along with the results of her initial research, she could gently suggest that she would try to help him sell his products to the more than two thousand assisted-living properties her company owned and managed.

Here, Bella received welcoming signals of inclination from the start. The marketing director scheduled an initial meeting with her very quickly, and they happily laid the groundwork for several subsequent meetings. Based on the information he provided, Bella became a recognized architect in the development of a strategic change in her company's business model. She recognized that she was unlikely to have been able to amass the kind of information she received from this critical enabler on her own, let alone do it in the space of six months she took to prepare her plans for change.

One of the key points to be taken from Bella's story is that you don't want to fall into the trap of believing that simply because people agree to talk with you or tell you they're interested in you, they're necessarily *inclined* to become critical enablers. Trust your instincts when you're face-to-face with a prospect. If someone appears reticent even though you try to explore variations on your gesture of progressive reciprocity, as Bella's first prospect did, it's likely that you're not going to get what you need. When that happens, cut your losses and move on to another prospect.

Availability

Important as inclination is for determining if a prospect is a critical enabler, availability is equally critical. It's all too easy to reach out to a hot prospect and ignore the signs that it isn't going to work because the prospect isn't available for you. What you need is someone who has time to help you, or who considers responsiveness a high enough priority to make time for you.

To determine whether someone is available, assess clues like speed of response to your letters, phone calls, and e-mails and the extent of follow-through on commitments to work with you.

People who score high on availability tend to

- Take your calls right away
- Respond to your voice and e-mail messages within a day or two
- Respond to your requests with dates and times to meet
- Give a time frame of their ability if their schedule does not permit an immediate meeting

People who score low on availability tend to

- Be hard to track down even if they initially seem inclined to help
- Require more than one call or e-mail to get them to respond
- Initially express interest in sharing contacts or information but have a hard time delivering
- Tend to be overcommitted and frequently report being busy
- Postpone or cancel meetings you've set up with them

Such unavailability can be episodic, but sometimes it is chronic. You may desperately want to talk to certain contacts and feel you are close enough to taste the value they could provide—but don't blind yourself to reality. The chances of making the connection may still be slim.

The word *available* describes those individuals who make it a priority to spend time exploring mutual interests. Availability directly relates to time and effort—yours and the other person's. It may not be worthwhile to invest time in waiting for someone to respond to you when there could be an even more valuable and *available* critical enabler right around the corner. From the very beginning you should decide how much time you are willing to invest in every prospect—and move on when that time expires.

This can be hard to do when someone at first appears to be able and willing to help. When communications switch from warm to cold, consider the burden of what you are asking for. If you've allowed someone to take control over your request for a third-party meeting, they may regret the offer later if it turns out to be harder than expected to deliver. The regret leads them to ignore your follow-up calls and messages, another form of unavailability. If you suspect this is what's happening, it may be worth one more try to get things back on track by offering to make the third-party contact yourself—but it may not be possible to get through if the gates are really shut. Again, if that happens, shrug and move on.

Charles, the "green energy" broker whose success story opens Chapter Six, got off on the wrong foot at first. His work as a commercial real estate broker had given him solid networking credentials. However, the people he knew were more apt to benefit from his new set of services than to help him put together a portfolio of companies and technologies to offer potential clients. His interactions with his network also tended to be highly transactional; that is, without a concrete exchange—say, buildings for money—there wasn't much else going on. His network tended to lack the sort of personal aspect that would make people willing to go out of their way to help him.

Given this state of affairs, Charles pounced on the concept of finding a critical enabler—someone who already possessed the intelligence he was trying to amass and would share it with him. His attention was drawn by a venture capitalist he knew only casually but with whom he felt he had a good enough rapport to approach as a potential critical enabler. His prospect welcomed Charles, and it looked like he was off to a great start. Unfortunately, despite an excellent progressive reciprocity referral to a technology transfer at MIT, Charles soon felt he was getting stonewalled. His calls weren't returned, or his contact was "out of the office," and Charles wasn't making significant progress toward his goal of identifying up-and-coming green energy technology companies. When it became clear that the prospect's unavailability was going to continue—making it unlikely that he would ever actually meet with Charles, let alone exchange information with him—we began to look for other prospects.

Like-Mindedness

Unlike inclination and availability, which can be difficult to assess without a direct encounter, *like-mindedness* is something you can often discover in advance. It's well worth looking for, as it can turn a potentially lukewarm contact into something bordering on the magical.

A like-minded individual can feel like an instant connection with you in one or more of several important areas:

- Age
- Cultural or geographical background
- Religious or spiritual beliefs
- Activities such as sports or hobbies
- Educational background, including pursuit of the same course of study or graduation from the same college
- Personality traits—being outgoing or reserved, for example
- Family status, especially if you have children of similar ages

Like-mindedness goes way beyond simply walking into someone's office and looking at the pictures on the wall to get clues as to interests or hobbies or friends. The like-mindedness component of the Right Person–Right Approach framework enables you to take the practice of identifying the right people to the next level.

In many ways like-mindedness gets lost in the shuffle in this day of impersonal Internet communication. Because of the false sense of security we tend to derive from the enormous number of contacts generated through Internet-based networking, it's easy to neglect taking time to get to know people as individuals. Although social networking sites make it easy to find people with similar interests, interests alone don't begin to guarantee that someone will have all the other attributes that would make for a good critical enabler. Indeed, that's one of the reasons it can seem so hard to pursue objectives in the current networking environment: having too many casual Internet contacts translates into not having the resources to do the necessary homework to be successful. And not doing your homework is one of the surest ways to waste a potentially productive attempt at exchanging value with another. So rather than trolling through your network looking for shared interests, it's useful to reverse-engineer the problem. That is, once you have found a potential critical enabler who seems to fulfill the rest of the right person criteria, then it's worthwhile to dive deeper in search of interests you share.

Some clients tell me they don't feel comfortable doing this kind of research. It can feel like spying on a contact. I certainly don't recommend that you do anything that makes you uncomfortable. But I'd also like to point out the many ways in which looking into people's backgrounds and discovering their interests is a normal and beneficial thing to do before you meet with them—it's the most primary of human needs to feel validated and understood, and your research is designed to help you satisfy this need and demonstrate a genuine interest in them personally.

With such an overwhelming number of people already posting their professional (and often personal) information on social networking sites, it's become a natural part of any business interaction to look someone up on Facebook or LinkedIn or another networking site. In fact, one of the first questions you often hear from someone you've just met is, "Are you on LinkedIn?" Having your information on these sites is the contemporary equivalent of handing someone a business card. If the person is not on one of the social networking sites, that might mean they are uncomfortable with putting personal or professional information "out there" for everyone to see, or the information they share is strictly business and it might be an indication that you should proceed cautiously— perhaps uncovering this information during your first face-to-face meeting rather than behind the scenes.

Keeping a close eye out for people's non-business interests often makes a big difference in how quickly they will identify with you. It predisposes someone to want to work with you if you share the same outside values and activities, whether it's fishing or bridge or martial arts. In addition, there is tremendous additional value to be gained by knowing more about the human side of the people you want to engage. Among other things, doing this kind of homework truly differentiates you from others who may be trying to approach this person. Although the cryptic, transactional approaches that I see people use seem so simple, all too often they are devoid of any human element or rapport building. Therefore, on this one dimension alone, it can be a breath of fresh air to your prospect if you simply acknowledge that you are kindred in some way other than business. Here's how it worked for one of my clients.

Richard was a partner in a leading international corporate strategy consulting firm, responsible for (among other things) the development of new business. In pursuit of this objective, he was talking with the CEO of a major credit card company. They'd had an initial meeting based on a referral, and Richard saw the prospect as having strong potential as a client. He knew this decision maker needed his company's services, but felt as though he hadn't been able to make the kind of progress he'd expected with him. When Richard met with me to discuss a second upcoming meeting, I asked him, "What do you know about this guy?"

"Well, I know about his job, of course," Richard replied, "and a little about his career history."

We immediately sat down to look up this potential client. One of the first things that popped up in our search results was that Richard's decision maker was deeply involved in a nonprofit organization whose mission was to support and encourage solid father-son relationships, especially among disadvantaged families. We got the very strong sense that his commitment to serving others was an important part of his identity. As soon as we began to understand this interest of his, I asked Richard if he knew anything about this. Without hesitation he said, "My uncle is involved with this same nonprofit organization, and he's recruited me to become involved as well."

Bang. Immediate connection. This identification of a key area of like-mindedness proved to be key to the success of

Richard's meeting with this prospect. In fact, it immediately transformed their relationship. A formerly unresponsive potential client was now suggesting they go out to lunch, on the strength of Richard's connecting with him on this very human level.

Being able to identify like-mindedness is one of the keys to delivering the "lightning strikes" relationships that further your business and career objectives.

What Next?

Discovering the inclination, availability, and like-mindedness of your prospective critical enabler is the final step in making sure you've identified the Right Person. Once you've completed the process of identifying, screening, and contacting your critical enabler, the next stage in the Right Person–Right Approach process is using the knowledge and contacts you acquire through your critical enabler to approach your target. Chapter Eight presents three case histories that illustrate how the Right Person–Right Approach method enables you to do that, not only to achieve your business objectives but also to use the framework to go beyond your original goals.

CHAPTER 8

Putting It All Together

We have now considered each of the separate stages of the Right Person–Right Approach method, one at a time. When you apply the method in pursuit of a business objective, though, you'll likely find that the process is actually more fluid than linear. The different stages in the framework almost invariably overlap one another.

For example, you may well find that you need to make gestures of progressive reciprocity very early in the development of your objective, even before you've identified a critical enabler, just to get through to the people who know the people who can help you. In addition, you're likely to find that, rather than a single referral to a single critical enabler, you may need to get several referrals to different people—each representing access to separate elements of intelligence or relationships that combine to have a catalytic effect on your progress toward your objectives.

In addition, rather than simply speeding up the pursuit of a simple business objective, the Right Person–Right Approach method often enables you to expand your objective substantially. For instance, if your initial goal is increasing sales by some percentage, you may find that following the method enables you to increase sales exponentially by reaching entirely new, untapped markets.

This chapter follows three individuals to illustrate how the stages fit together and overlap as they're put into action, and how finding the right critical enabler can take you to objectives that go far beyond your initial expectations. Further details appear throughout the chapter, but to begin, here are the people involved.

- *Sari*. Sari's search for a critical enabler opens Chapter Four, but her whole story has much more to show about how the stages of the Right Person–Right Approach method merge and support one another. As noted, she was an introverted research chemist in need of a new job and having trouble locating the kinds of jobs where she would shine. This chapter skips much of the detail up through her delighted recognition that she already had a tie to her ideal critical enabler—a microscope salesman who'd done more than a million dollars worth of business with her.

- *Arthur*. Arthur was developing a Web-based employee assessment application designed to enable employees to better align their values with those of the organizations for which they worked. He had worked in this field for a number of years at two large leadership development consulting firms, and he wanted to go into business for himself.

  Already a very well-connected, well-respected professional, Arthur was likable, thoughtful, and articulate, and in many ways the consummate networker, at least in terms of activity and volume. He had his own blog to deal with issues of professional interest, with a loyal following for his work. Unlike many of the people I work with, he was comfortable making (cold) phone calls, and he had relationships with a number of professional associates who would do what they could to help him. In other words, he had accumulated a good deal of "relationship capital." Unfortunately, even though he'd contacted many of his closest associates in search of the people and resources he thought he needed, his network had not come through with help for him.

• *Nina.* Nina worked for an international management psychology consulting firm as vice president for business development. This meant she had to deal with all of her fellow consultants, as the firm's products were too complex for a dedicated sales staff to handle—instead, the consultants were all expected to sell. Although this is a common new business development model in professional services, it wasn't working nearly as well as the firm would have liked, because most of the consultants were not natural salespeople, and they balked at being asked to promote their services to potential clients.

Nina was widely known and respected by her peers. Colleagues described her as a very good outbound marketer— that is, she sent out excellent newsletters, brochures, and Internet- and video-based materials—and she was also an accomplished seminar host. Her well-attended meetings were often a source of new business for the firm. As business development vice president, however, she was pressured to find other sources for new business leads.

How Do You Make the Method Work?

It's useful to keep a number of principles in mind. First, once you've articulated your macro objective, you need to keep focused on it without trying to keep it frozen in its first form. This will allow you to notice how it evolves as you build your frame of reference about the objective from each conversation. Because this process is designed to produce quantum advances in the knowledge base you depend on for achieving your objective, each new critical enabler you target represents an opportunity to both refine and expand your objective. So *focus* is the key to applying the Right Person–Right Approach method to achieve your career and business objectives.

Second, the Right Person–Right Approach method can lead you in unexpected directions. It's important not to rule out anything when it comes to identifying your critical enabler—people seemingly far afield from your target may provide an end run that takes you straight to your decision maker. Although the seemingly shortest path may appear most obvious, it is all too often full of hidden barriers and obstacles. In the end, you wind up with far less from the referrals than might have been possible.

Third, in many cases as you achieve your macro objective you might find that it leads you beyond what you'd expected. Your macro objective can actually be a springboard to go far beyond your original goals. The three stories we follow in this chapter will help you get a sense of just how powerful understanding and applying the concept of the critical enabler can be.

Preparation: Decide Where to Look

In the beginning, each of our three protagonists was looking for success in all the wrong places—or at least in the wrong way, driving straight ahead on their own, without attempting to automate or to delegate the legwork.

Sari

Sari started out by sending her résumé to any company that seemed likely to have a chem lab somewhere on the premises. Her operating question was basically, "OK, what companies are looking for people who do the kind of job I'm seeking?" Unfortunately, she was asking about jobs at a time when the job market was far from booming, and it is not surprising that the response was disappointing.

Arthur

Arthur knew what he was looking for: a Web designer, an editor, a webmaster (depending on the capabilities of his designer), possibly a financial partner, and possibly someone to help him run the business once he'd gotten it launched. He figured he'd have to engage many different sources to fill all these needs. In other words, he was going about the job of putting together a new company in much the same way everyone else does: by trying to do a lot of different jobs simultaneously.

When I suggested that he stop sending his talent specifications to friends, headhunters, and job boards (no matter how much that looked like the most direct path to the talent he needed), he brushed off the idea. Looking instead for one critical enabler who could really help him seemed way too indirect—like wishful thinking. Why, he asked me, should he waste time building relationships with people who didn't have exactly what he wanted? And if he was to hear of someone who *did* have everything he wanted, why wouldn't he go directly for it? I assured him that these were understandable objections, but I maintained that, in practice, an indirect approach can be the most efficient and effective way to achieve an objective.

Nina

Nina realized that her own success might cut her off from further development. She was so good at the kind of sales pitch she was used to that she'd gotten just about all the mileage from it that it could offer. If she was going to increase her sales still further, and help her fellow consultants to do likewise, she needed to approach her targets from a different direction.

The classic mistake most people make when they're beginning to pursue an objective is to focus on the end of the process. Although another of Stephen R. Covey's classic principles—"Begin with the end in mind"—is timelessly true, it can be deceiving if you view the networking path to that end as necessarily straight. Looking for a job? Logically, you'd ask who's got jobs to offer, as Sari did. Looking for help? Obviously, you'd advertise for it, as Arthur did. But business is not geometry. For example, had Sari asked her colleagues for referrals to people they knew who might have leads, she'd have begun to make progress much earlier.

This concept often seems counterintuitive, but it's central to the Right Person–Right Approach method, which is based on the observation that in human affairs, the straight road is often the longest distance between two points, not the shortest. If you want a lasting relationship, a singles bar is not the place to find it. If you want a job, responding to posts on job boards will drop you into an army of young people responding to the same posting, and your chances of being seen at all, let alone considered seriously, are very low. If you want to buy the perfect house, spending all your time visiting open houses means you miss out on the best ones, which get scooped up before the signs reach the lawn. In line with this, I advised Sari that, rather than broadcasting her credentials far and wide, she needed to be more specific with her targets.

Arthur's problem turned out to be the use of search terms that were—unlike those I usually see—actually too specific. Had he continued on the path he was intent on following, he'd have been inundated with unqualified candidate résumés. Screening and interviewing so many people for each position would have taken months.

Not only would this have been a very inefficient way to pursue his objectives of staffing his new business and possibly finding a business partner, but it might not have worked at all. He was simply being too direct—placing the burden of all the legwork, including interviewing and hiring key employees, on himself. Instead, he should have been looking for a critical enabler, someone who was already familiar with the process of developing a company from scratch—and better still, someone who had already done it at least once.

Nina's insight—that she needed to take a different approach—was the first and most basic step in preparation. Until she realized that her best efforts had topped out—that as good as they were, and of their kind they were very good, they were not enough—she couldn't begin to look for improvements. As in many situations, something that *almost* works or works fairly well can make it difficult to perceive something that might work better.

Setting Objectives: Know What You Want

Our collective wisdom constantly makes this point: If you don't know where you're going, you can't tell when you get there (or any place will do). If your only tool is a hammer, every problem looks like a nail. If you want something in the worst way, that's generally how you'll go about getting it. Nonetheless, it's surprisingly hard to stop and think about objectives. People generally live by the opposing maxim: I don't understand X, but I'll know it when I see it. In practice, objectives are both obvious and elusive at the same time. You can feel as though you know what you want, but if you don't spell it out, you're leaving it to others to read your mind—and it is probably true that your mind isn't really made up after all. So, how did our three protagonists approach this task?

Sari

Sari realized she needed to take a step back and rethink things, because the broadcast-your-résumé approach had not produced positive results. That meant that her macro objective—find a job—wasn't accessible, so we had to break it down into micro components in order to find someone who could lead her to the decision makers she needed to get in front of. To do that, we had to figure out what knowledge gaps were keeping her from finding the right person. So she started by describing her ideal working environment in great detail: the kind of laboratory, the types of projects it worked on, the technology it employed.

Arthur

Arthur realized that he didn't have a macro objective at all. He'd bypassed the macro stage and gone directly to a number of micro objectives. Unfortunately, even if he hired a headhunter to help him find a Web designer or an editor, he would still be conducting a very haphazard search, one that would demand a great deal of his time. Best case, he'd have to interview perhaps dozens of candidates, just to find one whose résumé came close and who appeared to be congenial—a process that quite likely would lead him to discover that he still hadn't found what he was looking for. Arthur needed to step back and refocus on his overall objective—a well-balanced and highly qualified staff that could make a success of the company he was building—and to find that, he needed help from someone who really knew the market and the common denominators among the various functional specialties he sought.

Nina

Nina started by asking me, "What companies do you know that need organizational change management consulting?"

My answer didn't help her much: "Perhaps 'everybody'; perhaps 'nobody.'"

The problem was, Nina was framing her search in the wrong terms. She was focusing on the state of mind of the decision makers at her potential client companies and essentially saying, "Get me in front of decision makers at companies that need organizational change management consulting services on a large scale." Because she'd framed her objective as "make another sale," her results depended on decision makers' giving her a call when they needed her. That meant she was not in control of the process by which she was trying to realize her business objectives. She was broadcasting material to thousands of targets and trying to build relationships with every one of her potential clients individually, and that meant she had to repeat the same "contact, present, and follow up" process with all of them, one at a time.

She needed to rethink how she was expressing her needs. She'd homed in on a micro objective—her audience—when she really needed to step back and ask, "Who has the answers to the question 'What companies need the services my firm provides?'"

Sari's story illustrates an important component in identifying an objective: be very specific when defining the knowledge you need. And one key to her success is that she was able to articulate very clearly precisely what her needs were, what she was looking for. Because she wanted advice about labs and not just a list of labs, she was able to save herself the dozens, if not hundreds, of phone calls that she would have needed to get in to talk with each of them. Framing her objective properly led her to someone who could introduce her to the right people and, fueled by a great referral and enough background information, approach them in the right way: demonstrating knowledge that opened doors immediately.

Your macro and micro objective statements are a crucial part of the process of putting together Internet search terms and querying trusted advisers who can provide honest feedback as to the vagueness or over-specificity of what you are asking. In other words, if you're defining your search terms too narrowly—if you find you're looking for six or eight different types of resources, as Arthur was doing—you need to step back and recreate a macro statement. You need to remember that you're not really looking for resources; rather, you're looking for someone who has the *knowledge* of those resources and who can direct you to them. You're trying to define a critical enabler, and you need to construct your objective statement with that end in mind.

Another key point in these stories is that a properly defined set of objective statements makes it possible to redefine objectives and aim much higher than may originally seem possible. For example, when Arthur first set out to staff his start-up, he was looking for "a Web designer and probably a webmaster." In other words, he was looking for, in sports terms, "a utility player"—someone who could do a workmanlike job on the immediate tasks. He'd set his goals fairly low, and hundreds of people on the market could have met those specifications. This may seem like a rich field—but it's more like a pile of manure: useful as it is, you don't want to sift through it by hand.

So don't let yourself worry about aiming too high. It isn't productive to ask, "What if the ideal candidate for the employee or partner I'm looking for doesn't exist?" or "What if my ideal employer doesn't exist?" Instead, aim for the best possible outcome. Even if you find you can't achieve it, you'll still very likely end up in a much better place than you would have if you'd aimed lower.

This argues, again, for keeping your focus on your macro objective. The point is that in seeking to accomplish any career or business objective, you need to articulate your objective in such a way that you're aiming for the best possible outcome. Don't start with low expectations; if you meet those, you'll likely fall short of your ultimate goal.

At the same time, you need to keep your objectives in perspective. To make progress toward her macro objective of finding new clients for her company, Nina couldn't go straight for it—asking for clients wouldn't get them to show up. When she rethought the path to that objective and started looking for people who would know where to find clients, that simple shift led her to a gateway to new opportunities that she'd never thought possible.

Identifying Critical Enablers: Find the Key

If you can define what you want clearly enough, it makes it much easier to see who could help you get it.

Sari

As noted in Chapter Four, Sari leapt almost instantly from (1) what the labs she wanted to find needed, to (2) who provided it to them, to (3) the perfect critical enabler.

Arthur

Once Arthur redefined his objective as knowledge rather than personnel, a whole series of useful questions opened up. He first asked—and I encourage you to ask yourself the same questions when you're working your way toward a job or career goal—"What do I really need to know here?" and then "What search terms can I come up with that will help me find out what I need to know?"

Because Arthur was developing a Web-based business, the Internet needed to be part of his search strategy. He was also looking to work in the area of *values-based assessment* and *leadership*, so those words would also be included. And because he'd be providing *consulting services*, he needed to use that in his search. When we searched on these terms, one of the first results was a company that specialized in the very type of values-based leadership development consulting that Arthur was pursuing—but with a business model just different enough to represent the perfect slight overlap in the services they provided, and to be truly complementary. A visit to its Web site yielded names of its key players, who almost certainly made a point of knowing just what Arthur needed to know.

Nina

Nina narrowed her search to these questions:

- Who makes it their business to know what companies are in need of services like ours?

- Who has developed relationships with my target market, but for somewhat different reasons than we've developed them?

It would have been great to find one answer to these questions, but (as is commonly the case outside real estate, finance, or dating services) no one made a profession of identifying clients for the specific service her company offered, and she was stuck. But there was a group of people who did make a business of knowing what she needed to know: other consultants in the same business! They were virtually the only sources we could come up with that would be likely to have the information she wanted to obtain. The obvious problem was that they were essentially her competitors, and it seemed like none of them would want to share that information with her, any more than she'd want to share it with them. Or would they?

When we parsed the situation further, we identified a subgroup of competitors who might very well be happy to share what they knew about the client base Nina wanted to penetrate. That's because not all of her competitors were as large as her company. In fact, a lot of leadership development consultants worked alone or with a small group, without support staff, and concentrated on providing services on a smaller, more individualized basis to departments and groups within the same large corporations Nina's firm served. Nina already knew several of the principals of these firms; she just hadn't been thinking of them as potential allies.

That was a good start, but she needed more names than she could come up with off the top of her head, so I suggested that she use the "watering hole" approach to generate the list she sought. In essence, the watering hole approach asks the question, "Where do the kinds of people I want to get in touch with hang out?" In other words, what organizations do they belong to, what journals do they read, and what Web sites do they visit?

One of the first names we came up with as a watering hole connection was an independent consultants association. When we accessed its Web site, it was clear that this was a key to identifying her new source of critical enablers. In this case, we needed to be able to screen these independent consultants to determine which of them had the qualifications Nina was looking for in her potential business partners. We defined this group of smaller independent consultants as people who provided services similar to those of Nina's company but on a smaller scale, to anywhere from one to five flagship clients, and who we suspected were regularly exposed to opportunities for similar types of consulting on a scale larger than they were capable of handling.

Our first task was to determine who they were. Rather than ask for the names of small consulting firms that provide organizational change consulting services to corporate clients, we returned to the basic question, "Who makes it their business to know who these people are?" The answer we came up with was the Organizational Consultants Development Network. Now we needed to ask, "Who in the OCDN makes it their business to know which of its members provide the kinds of consulting services Nina's company provides?"

The questions that lead you indirectly to people who can help you achieve your business objectives can cover an extraordinarily wide range, and finding them is frequently a very interesting creative challenge. Articulating the objective in such a way that it's broken down into specific steps is the key, not only to success but to *efficient* success. It's the way to save time and to ultimately attain your goal. Taking this approach is one of the reasons the

Right Person–Right Approach framework saves so much time in the pursuit of career and business objectives.

Nina, for example, later expanded her search from providers of small-scale services along the same lines as her own to providers of products likely to be used by companies in a position to hire her. The watering hole approach continued to prove its utility, too—once you figure out what sort of people you want to meet, the first thing to look for is where they hang out. Besides organizations, look at speaker rosters for professional conferences and meetings. In most cases, the people who are actively involved and well respected in their fields will also be the ones chosen to share their knowledge and best practices with conference attendees. And stick with what works; there's no reason to reinvent the wheel every time you're looking for new business partners. It's much better to work with others who have not only perfected the wheel but improved it so that it rolls along effortlessly.

I look at the search as exploring a sort of huge Venn diagram—the one that shows a bunch of intersecting circles. Each macro criterion in your search can be represented as a separate circle, and the best prospect for a critical enabler is the person who touches the most circles. But as you cast about for possible critical enablers, remember Nina's experience: don't eliminate any category of people from your search; you can find common ground in surprising places.

Obtaining Referrals: Get a Foot in the Door

In the abstract, the whole idea of getting referrals can seem forced and off-putting. It can feel as though the people who could serve as critical enablers are way out of reach, and even the people who could introduce you to them may seem unlikely to be willing to talk to you. Nonetheless, this phase of the Right Person–Right Approach method almost invariably turns out to work smoothly, much to the surprise of the many naysayers I've converted.

Sari

Sari had discovered that she was in the happy position of knowing her ideal critical enabler. The question was the answer: as soon as she asked what her target labs used and who supplied it to them, the name leapt to mind.

Arthur

Once he had the name of a company in a business very similar to the one he wanted to develop, Arthur queried his network in a very different way. Instead of asking his network whether they knew any Web developers or editors or people possibly interested in partnering in his business venture, he asked them a very specific question about a specific company that looked interesting to him.

Within a day one of his contacts got back to him saying that she knew the vice president of business development of the company Arthur had found. She further told Arthur that her contact, Mark, had been involved in several start-ups over the past ten years or so. She gave Arthur a referral to Mark, backed up by additional information about him, and Arthur contacted him immediately by phone.

Nina

Nina found it easy to reach many of the smaller consultants she'd identified in her search for critical enablers, and she moved straight to developing the dynamite gesture of progressive reciprocity described in the next installment of her story. (As noted, the Right Person–Right Approach method often doubles back and moves forward on several fronts rather than proceeding in the sort of linear fashion that makes a story easy to tell.) Based on the success of that effort, we began to look for ways to expand the new corps of critical enablers beyond the initial group of small-scale service providers. Asking, "Who *else* makes it their business to know the companies likely to need the kind of services Nina's company could provide?" we made the jump from service providers to vendors. The same group of potential client companies not only purchased consulting services similar to those Nina's firm provided, but also purchased products, including training materials and assessment tools, that helped them carry out their organizational development aims.

Nina's search on the term "professional organizations corporate training" produced very useful leads—including, among the first twenty-five results, more than a dozen professional organizations specializing in corporate training and training materials development and delivery as well as announcements of upcoming conferences and minutes of past conferences. Nina was familiar with most of them; she simply hadn't thought of them in relation to her own business. That is, she hadn't expanded her "universe of discourse" to include this category of potential business partner, so she hadn't been reminded of the large number of her associates who might be interested in partnering with her company for everyone's mutual benefit.

Nina called a few of the Organizational Consultants Development Network members she knew and asked if they knew and could provide her a referral to one of the board members of the organization. Almost immediately she received a "yes" response from one of her contacts who knew the OCDN's membership chair, and she used the referral when she called that person.

The key to getting referrals is to begin with the right question—and that is almost never going to be any form of "Do you know someone who can give me exactly what I want, based on my macro objective?" That approach puts the one you're asking for a referral on the spot, expected to answer a question to which they simply don't have the *direct* answer. The answer to "Who do you know that needs X" is almost always going to be "Nobody, but I'll keep an eye out"—followed by nothing but silence. The one you hit up for a referral will be worrying, *Suppose the suggested source doesn't come through for you? Suppose the suggested source gets irritated about being offered up for something that seems inappropriate or unobtainable?* Instead, you need to begin with a very clear and specific request for an introduction to someone who knows the sort of people who can provide the answer to your question.

The watering hole approach is especially effective at this stage—it's altogether unthreatening to ask where the sort of people you want to find hang out, or to get introductions to one or another of them once you're in the right place (either physically or via social media). Once Nina began focusing on potential critical enablers who made it their business to know the key training and evaluation companies and which of them might be interested in partnerships designed to extend their limited capabilities, progress soon followed. This thought process is essentially an adaptation and application of corporate channel partnership and alliance theory to an individual scale—throwing away the traditional do-it-yourself mind-set for sales, fundraising, job search, and other objectives and adopting a mind-set that enlists other people with shared interests.

Developing Gestures of Progressive Reciprocity: Make It Worthwhile to Help

Sari

Sari knew a sales rep who'd be ideal as a critical enabler, and she didn't need a referral to him, so we moved straight to figuring out what she had to offer in return for his help. It seemed very likely that he would be pleased to have someone well-disposed to him and his company in the sort of influential staff position she was seeking. Here is the e-mail message she sent to him:

Dear _____,

You may recall our meeting about five years ago when I was a member of the procurement team from _____ _____ company tasked with purchasing spectrometers for our laboratory.

(Continued)

You recently came to mind, as I'm looking for a position in another company, and it occurred to me we could easily help each other. The companies in my target market are the same as yours. Hence I was wondering if you saw the mutual benefit of selectively referring me to the people directly in charge of hiring for the labs I'm targeting, and sharing any information you're at liberty to about their specific needs. That would allow me to approach them more intelligently than I'm currently able.

I'm also hopeful this could be an opportunity for you to be perceived as providing added value by referring a well-qualified candidate. Of course, I would also do anything I could to advance your interests at any of these companies.

I'll follow up shortly to see if my logic makes sense to you.

Best regards,
Sari

Arthur

Because his new contact, Mark, was a vice president of business development and had an eye for start-ups, Arthur needed very little by way of a gesture of progressive reciprocity to encourage him to talk. His own thoughtful preparation and clear intent to develop a business represented an attractive enough opportunity that anyone Mark referred would likely be grateful. Mark really did make it his business to know everyone and everything about the field Arthur was interested in, and advising Arthur put Mark in a position to build relationship capital on several fronts.

Nina

Nina recognized that the smaller consulting firms in her field didn't have the resources to take on the kinds of larger jobs that Nina's company was capable of handling. Nonetheless, they were probably aware of many opportunities that they were too small to take on, and if she approached these independent consultants, they might be willing to become, in effect, the sales staff her company didn't have. They might very well be willing—say, in exchange for a finder's fee—to steer their corporate clients to Nina's firm when potential projects that were larger than they could handle came to their attention.

Nina therefore suggested that they might consider entering into a formal referral agreement by which the Organizational Consultants Development Network could hand off larger projects to Nina's company in exchange for referral fees for both the company recommending the project and the OCDN, while Nina's company sent business to the OCDN and its members if the scale was more appropriate for them. A formal agreement was developed and signed that outlined the framework of their referral relationship, which was formalized as the Business Development Network. The mission of the OCDN was to help the development and careers of its members and to add real value, so the gesture was perfectly in keeping with the OCDN's charter.

Progressive reciprocity needn't be too elegant and obscure. It's pleasant to be able to come up with connections or social gestures that will warm prospective critical enablers' hearts and enlist their assistance, but sometimes the way to their hearts is through their wallets. Nina, for example, didn't have to get too creative in coming up with a persuasive gesture—cold hard cash was the only incentive needed to motivate the smaller consultants, who quickly scrambled to find new business leads for her. This kind of gesture isn't always wise or even legal—don't try to enlist your Congressional representative's assistance this way—but an ongoing and mutually rewarding financial arrangement can work. That said, while a viable option, I do find the most natural reciprocal relationships occur organically without the artificial stimulus of money.

Let's return to Sari's message, because it is worthy of study. It illustrates two actions that I recommend everyone take:

- *Establish the connection.* This is the place for a referral, if that's what you're using to make a connection, but Sari didn't actually need a referral. Instead, her message reminds the sales rep of an earlier contact, when she was a member of her company's procurement team for spectrometers. (She didn't have to remind him that their interaction had resulted in her lab's making a $1 million purchase from his company. That's the sort of thing people remember!)

- *Offer bait.* Sari made it clear that it would be beneficial for the sales rep to advise her. On one hand, the advantage was built into the contact; if he referred her to the right kinds of places, the laboratory management would be glad to know he was thinking of them so intelligently, and the one that hired her would be especially glad of the assistance in finding someone they needed. And on the other hand, once she was hired, she'd be in a position to encourage the lab to view his company's products favorably—a quid pro quo more subtle than Nina's, but just as real.

And sometimes the opportunity for reciprocity is so clear that you barely need to mention it. When you locate a prospective critical enabler whose interests dovetail with yours as neatly as Mark's did with Arthur's, it takes very little explanation. Indeed, your main task is to adjust your own thinking—you truly are doing a favor by making the connection, not just asking for one, and the clearer that is in your own mind, the easier it will be for your prospect to recognize.

Making Sure You Have the Right Person

Sari

Sari's sales rep instantly understood that Sari was clearly proposing something of mutual benefit for both of them, and he answered her message at once. He was warm and forthcoming from the first, very generously sharing not only a list of the decision makers in the labs at the companies Sari was interested in, but also identifying which ones would be best to approach and where they were regarding need for personnel. He also gave her express permission to use him as a reference in approaching these companies. Sari and the sales rep further discussed key projects that each of the companies was involved in and how it made sense that she and he could and should help each other.

Arthur

Arthur and Mark found common ground right away. It turned out that, just as Arthur's referring party had thought, Mark knew the business Arthur was interested in inside and out: he knew values-based assessment and leadership training, and he knew the companies that were interested in obtaining those services. Although Mark wasn't available to work with Arthur himself, he had worked in the area of values-based assessment and was in touch with a whole community of people across all functional skills areas—including executives, marketing specialists, and computer programmers and Web designers—who had extensive backgrounds in this niche.

In particular, Mark identified someone who not only had the functional skills Arthur needed in a chief technology officer—including the ability to put together a staff for a start-up—but who also shared a background in and passion for values-based assessment.

Nina

Because Nina had keyed into organizations that were essentially set up to promote the kind of thing she was proposing, she found that she really didn't have to work to engender willingness.

Surprisingly often, prospective critical enablers are just as engaged and pleased to help as the ones Sari, Nina, and Arthur consulted. You need to think about the inclination, availability, and like-mindedness of any given prospect, but most of the people I work with find that their selection criteria have brought them to the right person—or at least, *a* right person. Where they run into resistance, like Bella (the customer service VP in Chapter Seven), they often realize that their first choice was not actually the best one available to them. If that happens to you, it's OK—just move on to the next prospect and don't succumb to the temptation to go back to your old ways.

The main thing to do when you communicate with each prospect is to *pay attention*. For one thing, it's rewarding in itself—in today's social climate, simply being focused on by someone who is genuinely looking for ways to help can be as welcome as water in the desert. It also will allow you to see signs of growing or declining interest and guide you to refine your offer of progressive reciprocity—or to thank your prospect and move on.

Going for the Gold: Enough Enabling; Let's Make a Deal

Sari

With referrals and inside information from the sales rep, Sari approached the five companies she found most attractive. She displayed specific knowledge of each company by writing, "Dear [decision maker's name], I was referred to you by [sales rep's name] from [sales rep's company]. I understand that you face some unique challenges in your polymer chemistry lab"—followed by outlining the salient issues for that specific company and her accomplishments that were most relevant to those areas.

Flush with newfound confidence, she felt no hesitation in picking up the phone and following up with each of them several days later, something she wouldn't have thought of even a few weeks earlier. Every one of her five prospects invited her in for an interview, and three of them offered her a job.

In an important sense, her Right Person–Right Approach job search became for Sari not just a career-changing event but a life-changing one as well, because she realized she could apply the principles she'd learned in her job search to virtually every other business or career objective she sought. The entire process, from preparation to settling into her new lab, took one month.

Arthur

Once he talked with Mark—a critical enabler who knew the industry and the players inside and out—Arthur learned that he could set his sights much higher than picking up a few utility helpers. He could actually add elements to his wish list he had never thought possible. Not only were there competent people who could both program and design out there, but some both met the job spec and shared Arthur's values, and could thus provide much more than simply computer expertise. Once his eyes were opened, Arthur found that the real possibility of achieving his objective—and achieving it very quickly—was within reach. He was able to move ahead within a couple of weeks on a project that might otherwise have taken up to a year to get off the ground. The chief technology officer he eventually hired was able to put together a staff to handle every one of the separate functions Arthur had initially said he needed, allowing him to accomplish all of his original micro objectives with a single hire.

Nina

Working with the membership chair of the Organizational Consultants Development Network, Nina was able to vet a number of the smaller consultants on the OCDN's membership rolls, and she came up with a very select list of six of the best-connected, most highly regarded consultants, to which she added two others that she had already identified from her own network.

With these select consultants, she formed what she called the Business Development Network, made up of smaller independent consultants who were out in the field, working with the very companies Nina's firm needed to reach. Because they were already working with major corporate clients, they were gathering valuable intelligence about their consulting needs. When they couldn't handle a job on their own, they were happy to be able to refer the client to Nina's company in exchange for a percentage of the revenues generated.

Her company's workload snowballed as a result, to the general satisfaction of all concerned. Within the first month, it landed a major project based on a referral from one of the new Business Development Network affiliates. Each of the consulting firms and suppliers that joined the network served as an ongoing critical enabler, providing invaluable intelligence and referrals to Nina's company and generating an ongoing stream of successes rather than one big win.

Each of the three people discussed in this chapter achieved the original objective and then some. Sari learned both where to look and what to point out about her background and abilities to differentiate herself from the flood of jobseekers. She didn't even need to send a résumé with her initial communication, because she knew what mattered most and could put it into a letter. In short, she took charge of the situation rather than passively sending out generic e-mails that would most likely end up in a folder in the filing cabinet of the companies' HR directors.

That is a common feature of the Right Person–Right Approach method; it makes it possible to stop deluging prospects with information in the hope that something will strike a responsive chord. The brevity and impact of the resulting message is itself part of its success, because the less labor you demand of a contact, the more likely you are to get what you want.

One of the things that I find most instructive about Sari's story is the way the experience changed Sari herself. She began with low confidence, uncertain of her English language skills and uncomfortable reaching out to people she didn't know well. As she gathered valuable intelligence from her critical enabler and began to realize this would enable her to differentiate herself from her competition, her confidence grew and grew.

Arthur's success was rooted in developing and focusing on a macro objective, setting aside the numerous micro objectives that he began with. It illustrates the importance of starting with the highest expectations—something I see over and over. If you don't aim for what you really want, you probably won't get it. For example, another client in a position much like Arthur's told me, "I want a whole team." And sure enough, a critical enabler referred that client to a whole management team, just laid off as a unit, who turned out to be perfect for the start-up she was putting together. So begin by articulating the ideal you'd like to realize, not some intermediate step that will get you only halfway to your finish line.

Nina discovered what was essentially a new business development model—not one new sale or one source of new sales but an expanding network feeding business to her company. By following it with an open mind, she found that the Right Person–Right Approach method allowed her to redefine her objectives on an ever-larger scale.

What Does It All Mean?

The Right Person–Right Approach method really is a fluid process. It's easiest to understand the elements that make it up if they're addressed as separate steps, but in practice you will find yourself looping back and doing things similar to what you've done before, but on another level.

Another thing you'll discover as you put the Right Person–Right Approach method into action is that it opens up new fields of inquiry and new objectives that you hadn't realized existed before. Although Nina began with the objective of increasing sales, it became evident, as she went through the process of developing new sales leads through working with her competitors, that there were other possible avenues for expanding sales that she was just discovering. In fact, Nina found she was just scratching the surface in expanding her company's opportunities.

Finally, although it's important to set your goals high, it's also important to understand that just randomly broadcasting well-articulated objectives rarely, if ever, will help you to realize such high expectations. The second key to Arthur's success is that, once he'd articulated his macro objective, he kept his focus on that objective. He used his well-articulated objective to find a critical enabler, someone who really knew the market and could actually match Arthur's specifications to real people in the marketplace. Keeping your focus on your macro objective to find the right critical enabler is one of the most important keys to achieving the best possible result.

Pursuing a business objective can feel like a matter of life and death—without the job, the funding, the information required to accomplish a project, you may face true hardship. So it's not easy to keep your spirits up, especially if—as often happens in today's economic conditions—the hunt drags on and on. Nonetheless, it can turn into a good game. I've seen it over and over in the context of the whole range of business and career objectives; once someone begins to apply the Right Person-Right Approach method, the obstacles become challenges that can be addressed. Reaching the objective starts to look like a puzzle with known pieces—and everything falls together neatly. As discussed in Chapter Nine, once you frame your objective clearly and take control of the process, you can proceed with confidence.

CHAPTER 9

Conclusion

USING THE RIGHT PERSON–RIGHT APPROACH
METHOD TO GAIN CLARITY, CONTROL,
AND CONFIDENCE

Although the Right Person–Right Approach method concentrates on providing you with a framework, a set of steps to follow to achieve your career and business objectives, the ultimate benefits go far beyond that. In three words, what the framework gives you is *clarity, control,* and *confidence.* It enables you to become absolutely clear in the statement of your objectives, to gain control over the process of achieving a business objective, and, because accomplishing the first two objectives is so empowering, to gain confidence you won't find in any other approach to achieving business success.

Why Pursue Clarity?

Arguably, the single most important thing you must do in implementing your personal Right Person–Right Approach process is to articulate your objective as clearly and completely as possible—that is, with *extreme clarity.* As I've said earlier, I often meet people who have at best a very hazy and general idea of what they're seeking to accomplish. Even those who are crystal clear on where they want to wind up tend to have little idea of the landmarks they need to reach along the way. In fact, I'd say that not truly being able to articulate their objectives—which translates to not knowing how to describe what they want clearly enough to get help—is the single most glaring shortcoming people face.

I see people who, instead of gaining clarity about their objectives, operate on the general assumption that they'll know what they want when they see it. If they talk to enough people, they reason, eventually they will stumble upon what they are seeking. The amount of time I see people wasting—as they network like crazy with little or nothing to show for it—is staggering. I find it painful to watch so many people beating their heads against the wall, with ill-defined and untested elevator statements presented to so many of the wrong people.

Even those who have a pretty good idea of what they need often have framed their objectives in ways that lead them down time- and relationship-consuming rat holes. They're generally looking at the wrong targets—decision makers rather than critical enablers—and this leads them to go off in pursuit of ineffective linear objectives. When you begin to think in terms of finding a critical enabler, you'll find that you reframe your objectives, becoming more specific in breaking them down into smaller components. So instead of asking people where to find money or jobs or whatever you ultimately want, you recognize how talking to people who have intelligence about and relationships with your target is far more productive as a starting point.

When you begin to see your task as identifying "search terms," it's truly liberating. Testing those terms first enables you, often for the first time, to get clear on what you're looking for before trying to find it. You'll discover that if you can articulate your objective in terms that will produce a small and meaningful set of results on the Internet or will pass the trusted adviser test, you'll have achieved an important milestone in your Right Person–Right Approach strategy. I use the word *meaningful* advisedly: your search objective is not to produce as many results as possible, but to produce a small number of highly qualified results targeted to your specific objective.

Once you've achieved extreme clarity regarding your business or career objective, you'll find that it's the first step in enabling you to take control of the process. For one thing, it will allow you to tailor your description of your objective to your audience, including the aspects and the amount of detail that will make the most difference to the particular person you're talking to, without losing track of the whole. If you try this sort of on-the-fly adjustment without being solidly grounded in a core statement of your objective, you're sure to be perceived as being all over the place—too scattered to be safe to deal with. In that case, no matter how much prospective critical enablers may like you, they are unlikely to want to subject their prized contacts to you and your uncertainty.

How Do You Maintain Control?

Almost without regard to what their business objectives might be, people who follow conventional methods to achieve them find themselves inadvertently giving up control of the process. Often they don't even realize that they're giving up that control, or even that they might keep control as they progress toward their goals. If that's happening to you, you probably know it at some level—if you get that hopeless, helpless feeling when your fingers let your generic cover letter and résumé or proposal slip into the mailbox or the out-box, you're sensing that you're at the mercy of the system.

With the Right Person–Right Approach method, control is central. After you've gained extreme clarity on your objective and tested it out on one or more of your trusted advisers, your next concern is to assert control throughout a process that will constantly challenge you to relinquish it. To reduce your chances of losing control, be very selective in the people you work with, guide the process, and turn your investment toward a pursuit of mutual benefit.

These days the most common advice is to take a shotgun approach and network with everyone everywhere—supermarket lines, parties, social media sites, and so on—and those activities are all right if you enjoy them and they come naturally. No matter how much fun they may be, however, they are always random and usually slow; results can feel like magic when they happen, but magic may be a long time coming, and you have no control over its appearance. A similar batch of advice suggests you get résumés or business plans or proposals out to as many people as possible, but that's also essentially leaving success in the hands of others.

Your pursuit of your objective works much better if you focus on finding a critical enabler or two to help you. The thing about résumés, business plans, and the rest of the hopeful documentation that people prepare in pursuit of their objectives is that those who have to review them *are rarely happy to see them*. Even those recipients who have advertised for jobs or proposals, who may regard a big response to their call as a pleasing success, tend to have far more documents to look at than will fit in the time they feel able to allocate to the chore—and those who haven't advertised almost certainly have other work that they feel is more aligned with their own purposes. Either way, the first thing that comes to mind when faced with another document is "How can I avoid reading the rest of this thing?"

That may sound harsh, but the process of exclusion is simply easier than that of inclusion. Someone who is screening many prospective hires, vendors, or investments is consciously or unconsciously just as interested in reducing the pile in the in-box as they are in finding the best prospect. The last thing you want is to be evaluated by some screener who is forced by sheer volume to look for all the reasons not to consider you. When you take control of the process and arrange to go from hand to hand to your real decision maker, armed with enough information to make yourself stand out, you've sidestepped the lemming line. Others are waiting with formal requests, documentation, medical claims, documentation in hand at the door of some gatekeeper while you're sitting with your target and shaping your mutually productive future.

The thing to bear in mind is that almost invariably, someone reviewing résumés or proposals starts by sorting them into piles. There's one for the masses—the faceless, nonreferred hopefuls who get the same coarse and perhaps totally automated Boolean consideration. The survivors move to the bottom of the second pile, which is much smaller but still thick, and which starts with submissions from people referred by friends and employees. And finally there is the pile of one—the one who went to the right person with the right approach, met with the decision maker in a coherent and compelling manner, and now is in a separate class from everyone else vying for the resources, relationships, tools, or capital at issue. Which pile would you rather be in?

Avoiding Exclusion

The idea is to differentiate yourself—to invite your audience to evaluate you more on the basis of your approach and conduct than on the basis of what you can document that you have to offer or what you want. If you apply the Right Person–Right Approach method, you put yourself in a position to make a strong impression as someone who is well-informed, thoughtful, and worth talking to—definitely worth getting a call. When you control the process, you can shape and manage decision makers' perceptions of you and have your audience exactly where you want them. Intrigued, they respond by asking for more information, and you reply by asking if there is anything else they can share about their needs, challenges, problems, and interests that would allow you to offer more specific and tailored information about your proposal—that is, about your background for the job you hope to get, or about the business for which you seek funding, or the product you hope to sell, or whatever your objective may be.

Rather than sending a write-up on everything you've ever done or mean to do, crossing your fingers, and hoping your target sees the fit (and nothing to object to), you can build a clear understanding of which of the individual value propositions, benefits, skills, and accomplishments among the many you have to offer will resonate with that person's interests. But there's nothing secretive or manipulative about what you're doing. Your whole intent is to be candid and transparent and provide real value throughout the process, to the point where you can say straight out, "I'm happy to send what you are asking for. But I'd love to know a bit more about what you are looking for so I can specifically address what I have that suits your needs, rather than sending you everything in a generic form and leaving it up to you to see whether there's anything there you can use." As at the earlier stages of the Right Person–Right Approach method, you want to fill in the blanks as much as you can. Never leave it to others to perceive what you have to offer, because chances are they'll be looking for reasons to simplify you out of their lives rather than reasons to include you.

Minding Your Own Referrals

By selectively approaching people you've worked with your critical enabler to identify, you're dramatically improving your chances of success, not only because of the name recognition that constitutes a referral's inherent value, but also because you're not giving up control over the process.

Even where referrals are concerned—and this is an area where it's all too easy to lose control—it's best not to lead anyone to believe that you're asking them to risk their relationship capital by referring you to someone you want to contact. Introductions and brief heads-up calls from a referrer are welcome if volunteered freely, but in any case you want to make the primary contact or at least the main inquiry with the person you want to meet, so you should educate referring parties as to why it is in everyone's best interests to allow you and only you to forward your request, brochure, résumé, or other paperwork. Keeping the lines of communication in your own hands means that you not only maintain control but also minimize the burden of the request, making it much easier for the referring party to help you. Avoiding the overuse of someone else's relationship capital accomplishes the same thing. This means you're always sending your own message, and because you've honed that message down to a very concise and compelling one, it's important that you be the one to deliver it.

Remember, although your ultimate objective may be to get in front of many decision makers, you do that by consolidating the path to those decision makers, by identifying a critical enabler—preferably one person, at most two or three, except in unusual cases—who will enable you to *connect well* with decision makers. Working with a critical enabler means that you can acquire enormous amounts of information—information that will enable you to differentiate yourself from competitors for the same prize. That differentiation in turn gives you even greater control over the process of achieving your objective: when people see how well-referred, informed, and motivated you are, they also witness your initiative and value *demonstrated* by this very approach, which would otherwise have been hidden in the massive and unfocused documentation *proclaiming* such value that marks the traditional approach.

What Does It Take to Keep Up Your Confidence?

Simply put, realizing that you can control the process of achieving a career or business objective in a win-win way gives you a level of confidence that is otherwise virtually unattainable. No other networking method is as reliable. I've seen it time and time again—as people begin to apply the Right Person–Right Approach method, they grow much more enthusiastic about their prospects. They experience a new sense of options, and they enjoy the challenge of finding people who can really help them and approaching those people in a progressively reciprocal way that says—in actions rather than words—"Although I know you could help me, I want to figure out how I can help you first. In doing so, I'll then feel good about asking you for help, preferring an exchange of value rather than feeling as if I'm on my knees asking for a handout."

Indeed, if there's one characteristic that speaks to this change in attitude, it's the fact that people grow much, much more confident as their work progresses. And if there's one reason they're more confident than they've ever been, it's their realization that they're in control of a process in ways they never were before. They're no longer putting requests for help out there, willy-nilly, and hoping that someone will come across them and deem them worthy of notice. It is exciting to see the shift in attitude as people realize they know their target and know exactly what about their proposition will make the most difference. They also know what to leave out, omitting the extraneous information that in the past has diluted the impact of their most salient points, causing their propositions to lose impact or miss the mark.

It's tremendously empowering to know that you're not just shooting in the dark—rather, you're determined to offer something of value to the specific people who can help you most before you ask them for something for yourself. And the transformation of confidence that results from extreme clarity is not just a matter of how good you feel—it makes a difference in your relations with other people. Without being aware of it, the people you meet pick up on your emotional state, and if you're afraid or uncomfortable, you give off nonverbal cues that you don't really believe in yourself or your approach. This kind of tentativeness, however inadvertently you may project it, is fatal in terms of discouraging or scaring away help from others.

And when you truly believe in what you are saying and asking, that will come through just as clearly. So I'm always delighted when clients have refined their objectives well enough to tell me, "This really feels authentic" or "This really is *me*" or "Now I know what to ask." Once you have the clarity of knowing exactly what your objective is and you also know exactly who can catapult you toward it with the right referrals, intelligence, or both, you will exude confidence. It's infectious. You can't fake confidence in the hopes of reaping its benefits—but you can make it real.

Revisiting the example of Mary—the classic introvert—had identified the chief medical officer of a major hospital as a prospective critical enabler. She discovered that he was about to give a talk at a convention in a nearby city. The date was too close to leave time to even query her network to see whether she could get an introduction, so—going against type—she determined that she would attend his lecture and perhaps approach him directly with her proposal, even though she didn't have a referral to him.

After hearing him speak, she realized that her research into the speaker's subject meant that she could confidently ask if she could keep an eye out for any specific studies or reports that would support his findings. It suddenly clicked: she could be *a vehicle of information* rather than feeling the need to be *a vessel of knowledge*. She got her answer, and she did have something of value, which she sent him. From there, she again was confident enough to up the ante and ask for specific referrals and intelligence to her target organizations. The process now just felt natural to her.

When you change your focus from "getting a job" or "selling an idea" or whatever your ultimate objective may be and start thinking in terms of finding a person who knows the individuals or organizations you want to reach, understands their strategic goals and immediate needs inside and out, and will share that game-changing information with you, your entire outlook changes. As you enlist informed assistance and begin to gather detailed and important information about your targets, you too will find yourself doing things you never would have contemplated before.

It's a wonderful feeling. Not only are people far more receptive and able to help you when you are approaching them deliberately, with clarity and progressive reciprocity, but you will find you are genuinely excited to approach those who really can help. It no longer feels like a chore. Clients tell me "The phone is lighter to pick up" and say things like "Let me at 'em" and "This feels so *natural*." They can look at the process as a game: one of finding the best critical enabler and figuring out how to help them in ways that surprise them into being happy to help.

What's the Take-Away?

Twenty years' experience and thousands of successes establish that the Right Person–Right Approach method is truly transformative, conferring on those who use it a sense of empowerment that comes with the clarity, control, and confidence the framework enables. I know that as you progress through your own Right Person–Right Approach process toward achieving your personal career or business objective, you'll be able to add your success story to those of the clients I've had the privilege of working with, as they gained the clarity, control, and confidence to attain their goals. It has been my honor to see so many people help me build it, refine it, apply it, and run with it to achieve great things. I never cease to be moved by those who are inspired by this work and take the time to tell me about it.

If you make this framework work for you, please write to mystory@wellconnected.me and tell me *your* story.

ACKNOWLEDGMENTS

Of course, I never could have written this book without the enduring support of too many people to mention. First, I am eternally grateful to the hundreds of clients who have allowed me into that sacred place in their lives and careers. Their relentless prodding and encouragement to codify the lessons exchanged among thousands of coaching hours made this book possible. They saw the method to my madness.

To my family, who stood by me all the way. Bobbie couldn't have been a more understanding wife. The best role model one could ask for has been my dad, who inspired me with his love, dedication, and work ethic. Ann's input from the beginning through cover design was key. I hope my big sis Cynthia has an idea how much I appreciated her encouragement. And Mom provided me with much-needed emotional and nutritional supplements.

My Jossey-Bass editor, Genoveva Llosa, fully understood the impact this book would have on the lives and careers of so many hard-working people. Her belief in me and solid guidance allowed the magic to unfold within these pages. Über-literary agent Jim Levine was the first to affirm that I actually was onto something important. Writer Greg Lewis managed to capture the many wonderful stories, largely composing this book from our hours of transcripts. Developmental editor Hilary Powers, with her oh-so-fitting name, did the power-editing with grace and humor and was unfazed by the looming deadlines that felt so crushing to me. Maureen Wrinn added so much more than words to the spark that she turned into a flame within me. And many thanks to John Butman, who not only put up with my requests for advice, but then offered unexpected crystal-clear insights I didn't know enough to ask for.

The definition of a trusted adviser is Katie Rose Hope, whose crash courses on the inner workings of publishing enabled me to navigate the shoals of these to-me uncharted waters. Authors Cliff Hakim, David Roper, Paul Gillin, Amit Mukherjee, Pat Skerrett, and Nancy Ratey all showed me the many ropes of writing and publishing, allowing me to stay in the ring. Author Steve Goldberg turned the tables on me and doled out some of the best coaching I've ever experienced. Not only did Dana Rapoport's thoughtful and persistent inquiries—"How's the book going?"—force my perspective with the answer, but her referral to Zick Ruben (thanks again, Zick) led me to Jim Levine, a story outlined in this book.

I extend my appreciation to Ralph Roberto for the brainstorming use of Essex Partners' conference room and to thought partners Mike Kinkead, Mark Bonchek, Gregg Bauer, Michael Watkins, and Nat Welsh for shedding their bright lights on my path.

I also heartily thank the many others who offered me strength through their persistent questions: "How's it going?" or simply "How can I help?": John DiCocco, Rob Schwartz, Josh Reynolds, Gregg Bauer, David Cutler, Eric Cressy, Darla Hastings, Mary Rivet, Liz Cheever, Cam Brown, Paul McLaughlin, Steve Garfield, and Gregory Peterson.

Gordon S. Curtis is principal of Curtis Consulting, an executive transition coaching and agency firm. He has helped hundreds of top executives accelerate and achieve success at critical leadership junctures of company building, realignment, advancement, exit, and career transition campaigns. His clients come from top emerging and established organizations and institutions including AmEx, AOL, Boston Consulting Group, EMC, Fidelity Investments, Monitor, Bank of America, GE, IBM, MIT Sloan, JP Morgan Chase and Pearson, and Sun Microsystems. Previously, Curtis served as director of career services and alumni relations at Boston College Graduate School of Management. A sought-after speaker, he has also been interviewed for and featured in the *Financial Times*, the *Wall Street Journal*, the *Boston Sunday Globe*, and *Fast Company*, among other leading media sources. Curtis is a board member of GiveUsYourPoor.org and resides in Marblehead, Massachusetts.

Greg Lewis received his Ph.D. in English from Kent State University. He has taught at Kent State, St. Bonaventure

University, and St. John Fisher College. He is coauthor, with Charles Gant, of *End Your Addiction Now*. Lewis's commentaries have appeared in the *Washington Times* and the *Philadelphia Inquirer*, as well as on many Web sites. His work is anthologized in the college English textbooks *Language Awareness* and *The Norton Sampler: Short Essays for Composition*.

INDEX

A

Aaron, 147–148
Alyssa, 83–85
American Society of Association Executives, 85
Arthur: background information on, 171–172; developing gestures of progressive reciprocity, 190–191; identifying his critical enablers, 181–182; Internet search terminology to useful to, 182; making the deal, 196–197; obtaining referrals approach by, 186; resistance to taking indirect approach by, 174–175; selecting the right critical enabler, 194; setting objectives, 178
Articulating objectives: avoiding subjective language for, 67–69; desired outcomes for, 71–72; information-gathering techniques for, 70–71; refining your macro/micro objectives for, 56–57, 64–67, 180; Sari, Arthur, and Nina's approach to, 177–181; scenario on, 52–54; starting the process of, 54–56; useful search terms for, 66–67, 182, 187
Audience: assessing success with networking target, 48–50; identifying your current networking, 41–44; identifying your networking target, 45–46. *See also* Prospect organizations
Availability quality: description of, 154, 161–162; examples of critical enablers with, 162–164

B

Barry, 101, 102
Bell Labs/Lucent, 6
Bella, 158–161
Berkun, Scott, 8
Business objectives: articulating your, 52–72, 177–181, 182, 187; assessing your success in achieving, 46–48; confidence gained by controlling process of, 209; using extreme clarity to set, 201–203; macro and micro, 56–57, 64–67, 180; Right Person-Right Approach

method to achieve, 4–5; setting, 177–181; social networking limitations for, 7–8. *See also* Networking objectives

C

"Calling Bullshit on Social Media" (Berkun blog), 8

Career objectives: articulating your, 52–72, 177–181, 182, 187; assessing your success in achieving, 46–48; confidence gained by controlling process of, 209; using extreme clarity to set, 201–203; macro and micro, 56–57, 64–67, 180; Right Person–Right Approach method to achieve, 4–5; scenario on articulating your, 52–54; setting, 177–181; social networking limitations for, 7–8. *See also* Networking objectives

Carolyn, 97, 99

Celeste, 125–126

Charitable causes, 141–142

Charles, 163–164

Clarity: implementing Right Person–Right Approach through, 201; setting your objectives with, 201–203

Clayton, 101–102

Coattail comfort problem, 95

Colleen, 141–142

Communication: effective approach at professional events, 32–33; getting feedback from trusted advisers on your, 44; identifying your target audience, 45–46; positive outcomes of Right Person–Right Approach method of, 47–48; progressive reciprocity offer e-mail, 189–190, 192–193; undoing prior damage using the Right Person–Right Approach method, 50–51; of your own like-mindedness, 168–169. *See also* E-mails

Communication assessment: description categories to use for, 49; determining success in reaching target audience, 48–50; of your current audience, 41–44; of your message, 35–41; of your success/failure ratio, 46–48

Competitor news, 133–135

Confidence: benefits of expressing, 210–211; controlling your process to gain, 209; example of gaining and using, 211–212

Control: avoiding exclusion by maintaining, 206–207; minding your own referrals by maintaining, 208–209; over process of exclusion, 205–206; as Right Person–Right Approach method focus, 204–205

Covey, Stephen R., 6

Critical enabler needs: additional ways to identify, 145–149; doing research to identify, 114–116; finding a way to fulfill, 122–123. *See also* Progressive reciprocity examples

Critical enabler selection: availability quality

J

Jane, 22–23, 24, 43, 56
Jerry, 138, 139–140
John, 97–99
Jonathan, 127–128
Joseph, 22, 23, 24, 43, 56
Josiah, 92, 93
Judith, 119
Julie, 131–132

K

Knowledgeable element, 153
Korn Ferry, 11

L

Laura, 97–99
Like-mindedness quality:
    description of, 154, 164–165;
    examples of critical enablers
    with, 165; learning how to
    communicate your own,
    168–169; learning to identify,
    165–168
LinkedIn, 7, 33–34, 151–152
Lorrie, 111–113
Lower revenues (search term),
    66, 67

M

Macro networking objectives:
    description of, 56–57; practical
    process of creating micro
    objectives from, 64–67; role in
    Internet search and research
    by, 180
Mark, 190–191

Market disruption, 68–69
Mary, 143–145, 211
Matt, 108
Max, 122–123
Megan, 134–135
Mergers (search term), 66, 67
Messages: example of effective
    networking e-mail, 38–39;
    example of poorly written
    e-mail, 35–37; how to frame
    your e-mail, 37–38; identifying
    the audience of your, 41–44;
    of progressive reciprocity
    offer e-mail, 189–190, 192–193;
    questions used to assess your,
    40; tips on developing an
    effective, 39–41
Michelle, 70, 71, 72
Micro networking objectives:
    description of, 56–57; practical
    process of converting macro
    into, 64–67; role in Internet
    search and research by, 180;
    useful search terms to help
    articulate, 66
Misdirected messenger problem,
    94–95
Motivated element, 153

N

Networking: effective approach
    to professional events, 32–33;
    learning to reestablish old
    contacts and spark new
    contracts, 21; online social,
    7–9, 29, 33–34, 151–152; scenario
    on redefining 21st century,
    1–3; time-effective, 27, 33, 35;
    traditional methods for, 5–7.

progressive reciprocity focus, 117–118; on spinning your wheels at events, 27, 31–33; on what your networking goals are, 26, 28–29

R

Radtke, Warren, 11–12, 14, 15
Rapid growth (search term), 66, 67
Real-life challenges: articulating your objectives, 64–71; contacting referred person yourself, 103–105; creating an introduction to referral, 97–99; gathering information through referring party, 101–102; identifying your critical enabler, 80–83; learning critical information about critical enabler/organization, 86–90; screening a critical enabler, 83–86; when traditional referral process goes wrong, 107–110
Reciprocity: description of, 113–114; obligatory, 19. See also Progressive reciprocity
Referral management: contacting referred person yourself, 96, 102–105; gathering information through referring party, 96, 99–102; maintaining control over the, 208–209; making it easy for your referring party, 96–97; three features of, 96
Referral problems: coattail comfort, 95; misdirected messenger, 94–95; nonendorsements, 94

Referrals: creating an introduction, 97–99; losing control over process of, 107–110; maintaining control over process of, 208–209; from perspective of the referring party, 105–107; problems with traditional approaches to, 93–95; Sari, Arthur, and Nina's approach to obtaining, 185–189; scenario on getting a, 92–93; taking a better approach to, 95–96; three features of effectively managing, 96–105; watering hole approach to obtaining, 188–189. See also Critical enablers
Referring party: contacting referral yourself instead of through, 96, 102–105; gathering information through, 96, 99–102; making it easy for your, 96–97; referral process from perspective of, 105–107
Regulatory problems (search term), 66, 67
Rehberg, Ginny, 13–14
Rehberg Management Group, 13
Relationship capital, definition of, 9–10
Research: on critical enabler through referring party, 96, 99–102; on critical enablers' needs, 114–116; on critical information about organization/critical enabler, 86–90; helping people help you with, 70–71; macro and micro objective statements role in, 180; for selecting and engaging

195–196; obtaining referrals approach by, 186; selecting the right critical enabler, 193–194; setting objectives, 177–178, 179; traditional résumé approach taken by, 174

Services: disruptive products and, 68–69; providing news of the competition's, 133–135; strengthening the supply chain for a prospect's, 135–137

Social networking: description of, 7–8; Facebook for, 7; false sense of security from, 29; LinkedIn for, 7, 33–34, 151–152; "noise" of, 8; Twitter for, 7; understanding limitations of, 8–9

Supply chain: examining strength of your prospect's, 135; examples of progressive reciprocity related to, 135–137

Susanne, 107–109

T

Target audience: assessing success with networking, 48–50; critical enablers as

your, 43–44; identifying your networking, 45–46; questions to assess response patterns from, 45

Terrence, 135–136

Tim, 64–65, 67, 71, 72

Time-efficient networking, 27, 33–35

The Tipping Point (Gladwell), 155–156

Tony, 103–105

Trusted-advisers: assessing your past communications with, 45–46; getting feedback from, 44

Twitter, 7

Tyler, 86–88

W

Watering hole approach, 188–189

We Are All Self-Employed (Hakim), 106

Web sites: American Society of Association Executives, 85; Directory of Executive Outplacement Consulting Firms, 11; Gale directory, 85; Innovator's DNA, 6